Saving
Dogs and Souls

PATRICK METRO

Saving
Dogs and Souls

A Journey into Dog Rescue

ARCHWAY
PUBLISHING

Archway Publishing books may be ordered
through booksellers or by contacting:

Archway Publishing
1663 Liberty Drive
Bloomington, IN 47403
www.archwaypublishing.com
1 (888) 242-5904

Proceeds from the sale of this book will be used
to support golden retriever rescue.

ISBN: 978-1-4808-3329-6 (sc)
ISBN: 978-1-4808-3328-9 (hc)
ISBN: 978-1-4808-3330-2 (e)

Library of Congress Control Number: 2016948556

Print information available on the last page.

Archway Publishing rev. date: 8/16/2016

To Mary Ellen and all dog lovers

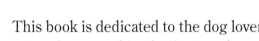

This book is dedicated to the dog lovers all over this
country whose combined efforts each year save more than
a million dogs that would otherwise be euthanized.

Contents

Glossary

IN THIS BOOK YOU WILL FIND A NUMBER OF terms with which you may not be familiar. Here are some brief explanations.

PTS: An abbreviation for "put to sleep" used by many animal shelters that euthanize dogs.

Rainbow Bridge: When a dog dies, it is said to have passed over the Rainbow Bridge and gone to dog heaven.

five-star dog lovers: The most passionate and dedicated class of dog lovers.

counter cruiser: A dog that puts its paws up on any counter where there is food and helps itself to a meal.

escape artist: A dog that takes any opportunity to get out and roam. It finds an open door, a hole in a fence, or a dropped leash, and off it goes on an adventure.

forever home: A final, loving home where a dog has been placed and presumably will live out the rest of its life.

foster failures: Fosters who bond with a foster dog in their care and decide to keep it rather than give it to an adopter.

permanent fosters: Fosters who care for a rescued dog until it dies, with the rescue assuming all medical costs.

Parade of Rescue Dogs

AFTER LUNCH, THE OWNERS GATHERED around, sitting on the ground and forming a large ring. It was mid-February and the weather was cool, so many slipped on light jackets. Under a bright Florida sun, Mary Ellen donned a headset that was wirelessly attached to a couple of large speakers and took her place in the center of the ring. She then called out certain owners and had them assemble with their dogs to form an inner circle. It was called the Parade of Rescue Dogs. These owners and their pets had compelling stories of rescue, bonding, and new life.

Once all the dogs were assembled, Mary Ellen had the owners parade their dogs around this inner circle. Then she introduced each dog and began to tell its rescue story. With some of the dogs, she had been the one to make the initial rescue contact, and just the sound of her voice when she called them up set them off. She could not start telling their stories until the dancing stopped and the hugs and kisses were exhausted.

Working without notes, she related in detail the circumstances of each dog: when it was brought into the rescue, where it was found, what condition it was in, and, in some cases, the heroic measures that were needed to restore the dog to health. She then outlined what had transpired to produce the happy and well-adjusted dog everyone was now seeing in the ring. Since Mary Ellen was often the volunteer who first came in contact with a dog in the rescue process, she knew firsthand all the circumstances surrounding each rescue, and she shared each detail with the other owners. What everyone was now seeing—a healthy, active, well-cared-for pet—in no way resembled the dog that was first brought into the rescue. Each story was a testament to the remarkable owners who had devoted themselves to saving these dogs.

Some stories were new and recent; others were not. It didn't matter that some people had heard these stories before—they never tired of hearing how abuse, cruelty, and abandonment had been overcome to produce a loving dog in a bonded relationship with an owner. They never tired of hearing how a dog and owner found each other and were completely devoted, or how unlikely this outcome was, considering the original circumstances.

One by one, each dog and owner in the ring became the focus of attention as Mary Ellen told their story, and each story ended with warm applause and smiling faces. Afterward, the adopters sat and socialized for hours, sharing anecdotes. This was what they looked forward to each year and why they'd packed their campers and driven for hours to be there. They didn't want it to end.

The Parade of Rescue Dogs was equally rewarding for Mary Ellen, who found it very satisfying to be surrounded by the dogs she had either rescued herself or played some part in rescuing. She knew how all their stories started, and seeing the dogs at the reunion closed the circle for her, because now she knew how their stories ended.

Some of those stories are told in this book. I can't tell all the tales of Mary Ellen's rescues over the years—there are just too many—but these are the ones that touched our lives in a special way. They are true stories from my wife's experiences in golden retriever rescue in northern Ohio and then in Naples, Florida.

The book is divided into two parts. The first part covers my wife's introduction to dog rescue as a volunteer with GRIN, a golden retriever rescue in Ohio. The second part details our move to Naples, where we started Golden Rescue in Naples, Inc., and my wife's work with a hospital ministry there.

Rescue Dogs and Rescue Organizations

THERE ARE MORE THAN THIRTEEN THOUSAND animal shelters in the United States, and each year approximately four million dogs are turned in to these shelters. Most are relinquished because the owner's place of residence does not allow dogs, because the owner does not have enough time for the dog, because of divorce or death, or because of behavior issues. Only 35 percent of these dogs are adopted out, and 31 percent are euthanized. Those dogs that are fortunate enough to be adopted—many of them saved from certain death—are termed "rescue dogs," and rescue organizations are primarily responsible for nursing them back to good health and placing them in forever homes. There are a vast number of rescue organizations in the United States, and the volunteers working with them number in the thousands.

A good resource for education of the golden retriever breed as well as finding a local golden retriever rescue organizations is the National Golden Retriever Club of America (GRCA). It is supportive to the rescue activities of the nearly 100 locally formed and administered golden retriever rescue programs throughout the country. The National Rescue Committee, a committee of the GRCA, does provide coordinating and networking NRC.org for those programs as well as developing literature, resources and maintaining a website http://www.grca-nrc.org/. This web site can help you find a local golden retriever rescue organization and through that rescue help you adopt a rescued golden retriever.

The size of rescue organizations varies greatly. You will find dog lovers who operate a rescue solo and independently, but the majority of dog rescue is done through rescue organizations. Some large rescues have more than a hundred volunteers. These rescues utilize over 8000 volunteers and spend close to 10 million dollars annually half of which is spent on veterinary fees. Women make up the vast majority of volunteers doing rescue work. While some rescue organizations take in any breed of dog, most are breed specific, manned by volunteers devoted to rescuing dogs of their favorite breed.

Rescue dogs come from various situations and sources, not just from animal shelters. Rescues also get them from veterinarians, local animal services, police departments, and any other entity that might have dogs turned in to it. In some cases, owners will contact a rescue directly and relinquish their dogs. Other dogs are abandoned—simply turned loose to fend for themselves, or left tied up outside an animal shelter or police station. Sometimes elderly people will suddenly require nursing care and have to give up their companions. Their families or caregivers cannot or will not take the dogs, which are then turned over to a rescue. Some families experience financial problems and can no longer afford their dogs. The list of reasons is vast, and circumstances vary, but rather than allowing the dogs to be put on the PTS list at a shelter or end up in another problematic situation, rescues bring the dogs in and eventually find them loving forever homes, giving them a new lease on life.

Those who adopt rescue dogs have their lives enriched as

well. They are true dog lovers. They experience the special bond that exists between a rescuer and the rescued. This is a unique bond, as anyone who has adopted a rescue dog will tell you. Many of these dogs have been abused or neglected; they come in grubby-looking, with poor coats, and quite often their eyes are dull and sad—the hallmark of an abused dog. They are not show-quality dogs and certainly do not resemble show dogs in any way. These dogs require medical care. Their spirits are gone. They are confused. (*Where is my owner? Who are these new people caring for me?*) Rescue volunteers are accustomed to this, and they know that given enough time and love, an entirely different dog will emerge. It is just the challenge dog lovers are looking for.

Everything starts when the rescue is alerted that there is a dog available or someone calls and wants to relinquish his or her dog. A volunteer goes out, picks up the dog, and drops it off at the office of one of the veterinarians who works with the rescue at a discounted fee. In many cases, the medical needs of the dog have been ignored, and so the dog is brought up to date on its shots, is neutered or spayed, has blood work done, has any tumors removed and biopsied, and has any other medical issues examined, with appropriate medication prescribed. Only after the dog has been cleared medically will it be put into a foster home.

Each rescue has an array of volunteers who provide foster homes. A volunteer will take the dog in for weeks, sometimes months. During this time, the foster observes the dog. Is it good with children? Does it get along with cats and other dogs? Is it an escape artist? Is it a counter cruiser? In time, the foster home will also uncover the dog's personality—its likes and dislikes—and when the time comes to place the dog into a forever home, it will be matched with prospective adopters. The foster volunteer has a say in approving any prospective adopter for the dog in his or her care. In many instances, the volunteer has the final say.

Sometimes volunteers become so attached that they cannot part with the dogs they are fostering, and they decide to keep them. They are referred to as "foster failures," a title they wear with pride. Although a foster is always given the first option to adopt, fosters usually do not keep the dogs in their care; they're just happy to see their charges go to good forever homes.

Fosters serve a valuable purpose. They are so important to a rescue. They know the dogs in their care better than anyone, and rescues realize that these individuals have a unique perspective as to whether a match is a good one that will work. Because of the foster system, few rescue dogs are returned after they have been matched with their new owners.

An adopter must sign a legal agreement stating that he or she will abide by certain requirements, such as providing a fenced-in yard and ensuring that the dog always wears a collar with identification tags. In addition, if the adopter has to give up the dog for any reason, the dog must go back to the rescue; the adopter can't just pass the dog on to someone else. These regulations may seem unusual or harsh, but rescues are devoted to the best interests of the dog, and if you can't or do not wish to abide by their rules, then you'd best look elsewhere.

During my oral/maxillofacial surgical residency, I worked in an orphanage, and the vetting process for adoptive parents there was very similar to what you'll experience as a prospective adopter at a rescue organization. You'll fill out a lengthy application listing all your previous dogs and the veterinarians you've used. The rescue will contact those veterinarians to find out whether you have been a responsible dog owner and whether they would recommend you as an adopter for the breed in question. When you clear that hurdle, a volunteer will make a home visit, asking a variety of questions. (Where will the dog sleep? Will it be allowed anywhere in the house?) Then the volunteer physically inspects things like your fenced-in yard and so forth.

If you pass all those tests, you've made the list of prospective adopters, and then you wait for an available dog to come into the rescue, one that is matched to you and your circumstances. Ask anyone who has adopted a dog from a rescue, and he or she will gladly tell you, "You won't believe what I had to go through to get this dog."

Rescues sustain themselves through fundraisers, donations, and adoption fees. Most rescue organizations are 501(c)(3) public charities as designated by the Internal Revenue Service, and any donations to them are tax deductible. The principal volunteers serve on the board of directors that runs the rescue.

Dog lovers display various degrees of commitment and zeal, but at the pinnacle is what I call the five-star dog lover. Dog likers cannot begin to comprehend the extremes to which dog lovers will go for their dogs. It is equally difficult to explain the depth of passion and devotion needed to qualify as a five-star dog lover. The following story illustrates that passion far better than I can describe it.

Saving Skidder

APRIL AND SANDY WERE TWO RESCUE VOLUN-
teers my wife, Mary Ellen, worked with in Ohio before we moved
to Florida. The three of them remained close and corresponded
often over the years. After we moved, April and Sandy started
a successful golden retriever rescue in Cleveland called Golden
Treasures Golden Retriever Rescue.

Not long after the women launched their new rescue, they
received a litter of golden puppies from the local humane society. The puppies had come from a backyard breeder and had no
socialization. The chances that they would be adopted through
the shelter were slim, and so the rescue took them in along
with their mother. After several weeks, the puppies had made
excellent progress and were being placed in forever homes. This
rescue did not ordinarily adopt to out-of-town applicants, but one
Michigan couple met their standards and appeared to be a good
match, so the rescue made an exception.

The applicants lived near Lake Huron, and in June 2011 they
made the four-hour trip to Cleveland with their other dog to meet
Skidder, the golden puppy. Their dog and Skidder got along fine,
and everyone agreed it was a good match, so Skidder went to
his new home in Michigan. After a four-hour return drive, the

couple pulled into their driveway. When they opened the car door, Skidder bolted out and ran off.

When the rescue learned that Skidder was missing, Sandy and one of her volunteers, Briget, made the drive to Lake Huron in an effort to locate him. His new family had been putting out food and had caught glimpses of him now and then, so they knew he was in the area. The volunteers alerted the local dog warden of Skidder's escape. Then they made a return trip and brought Skidder's mother to the area in an attempt to lure him to them. Skidder was staying in an area between two ravines, and the volunteers spent two days walking the area with Skidder's mother. However, they only caught a brief glimpse of him, and they had to return to Ohio without any success.

Briget and Sandy then rented a property next to one of the ravines, but the property had no accommodations, and so they returned with a tent and camping supplies along with a live trap. The area was rural; most of the houses there were used as weekend getaway homes. For the next four weeks, the women traveled to Michigan every five days, staying for two or three days at a time. On each trip, they set the live trap.

They quickly discovered that Skidder only came out at night, so their days were spent knocking on the doors of all the homes within two miles of where he had originally gone missing, as well as walking the beach and ravines, looking for signs that he was still in the area. At night they listened for the jingle of the tags on Skidder's collar. On several nights, they heard the jingle of his tags and the door of the live trap closing, but he somehow avoided being captured. The only animals caught in the live trap were raccoons and possums, which the women released. Once again, they returned to Ohio without Skidder.

Next, the volunteers constructed a special portable dog pen with a one-way door. They brought Skidder's mother, Roxy, and his brother Benson to Michigan, hoping that the familiar scent of Skidder's family would draw him out. It was mid-July by then, and there were swarms of biting flies along with temperatures in the eighties during the day. The volunteers were tired and miserable, but their thoughts were only of Skidder. In the mornings, they walked his family through the area, and in the afternoons, when the flies and temperatures became intense, they sought relief in Lake Huron. At night, a breeze from the lake cooled the air to the midsixties, bringing some comfort. The women would place Roxy and Benson in the portable dog pen each evening in the hope that Skidder would appear and go through the one-way door to reunite with his family. Sure enough, the jingle of Skidders' tags one night alerted them to his presence. His mother and brother began to whine, but Skidder did not enter the pen that night or the next night. After four days, the volunteers again went back to Ohio without Skidder.

The rescue contacted several dog behavior experts, veterinarians, and other rescue organizations to get advice, opinions, and ideas. They did a mass "Lost Dog" mailing to all nearby residents and local veterinarians; it featured Skidder's picture and offered a thousand-dollar reward to anyone who found him.

At this point, unfortunately, the relationship with Skidder's adoptive family became strained. The family chose to return legal ownership of Skidder to the rescue organization and discontinue assisting the rescue's efforts to find him.

Sandy and Briget continued to drive back and forth to Michigan whenever their work schedules and family responsibilities allowed, each time searching during the day and sitting quietly at night, looking and listening for signs of Skidder. They continued to use the dog pen and the live trap, putting strong-smelling canned food inside for bait. They also started putting out stuffed toys with his littermates' scent on them. By now it was August, and they needed to try something new. But what?

They searched the Internet and found a net launcher designed to catch large animals without harming them. They contacted the manufacturer and explained Skidder's story. Representatives from the company were certain the device would work. They directed the women to a YouTube video that showed it being used to catch a domestic dog. It looked promising, but the women would need to be within thirty feet of Skidder and have good aim. They ordered the launcher and began to practice using a very large stuffed dog.

Sandy and Briget returned to Michigan with renewed hope. For five nights they sat in various locations, listening for the jingle of Skidder's tags and hoping they were near a path that he traveled. On the last night, even though it was extremely dark, they saw a ghostly figure moving across the top of the bluff and could make out the shape of a dog and the faint glow of Skidder's light-blond fur. Briget aimed the net launcher and waited for Skidder to come closer.

He stopped twenty feet from her to eat the food they had put out. Briget shot the net and hit the target, but the net did not completely capture Skidder, and he was able to break away. They could hear him stumbling about, but it was too dark for them to see him. By the time they zeroed in on him using flashlights, he had escaped from the net, leaving it torn and tangled. Suddenly they realized that they no longer heard the jingle of his collar. His tags had come off; he could now travel around silently. Once again they went back to Ohio, disappointed.

A friend offered to lend them three wildlife cameras, which they placed on the property of a sympathetic older couple who were willing to help them capture Skidder. It was from those cameras that a pattern of Skidder's travels could be established. Sandy and Briget spent the rest of August and part of September sitting up at night with the net launcher and traveling the area during the day. Unfortunately, they never got a second chance with the net launcher.

It was now late September, and summer weather was coming to an end. A sense of urgency overwhelmed the rescue volunteers. They asked themselves whether Skidder could survive a winter living in the wooded ravines next to Lake Huron, and whether they could carry on the search for him during the winter months. Their efforts to capture Skidder continued.

By late October, it was too cold to sleep in a tent and sit out all night. Just as despair was about to take over, the retired couple who had allowed Sandy and Briget to use their property offered a warm bed in their home. Now, using hand warmers and wearing many layers of cold-weather clothing, Sandy and Briget were able to sit outside for three to four hours at a time, knowing that a warm house and bed would be available at night.

The search continued until late November, when the cold forced Sandy and Briget to suspend their efforts to capture Skidder. The retired couple offered to put food out for him every night, and so the volunteers felt some relief knowing that he would be able to eat. They left eighty pounds of dry food and three cases of canned food with the couple.

During November, December, and January, the women took day trips to Michigan to view the pictures from the wildlife cameras and then silently walk the ravines, looking for Skidder. They also continued to search for new ways to keep track of his activities and safely capture him. In mid-January 2012, Briget and Sandy returned to Michigan with a new idea.

As it was still too cold to sit out at night and the day trips to check the cameras were costly and time-consuming, they asked permission to install new cameras on the couple's property. These cameras were equipped with night vision and motion sensors, and what they detected could be viewed live over the Internet. The couple was very supportive, as by now they too were very committed to capturing Skidder. The new technology allowed Sandy and Briget to see Skidder every night making the same trek across the couple's property. He was still alive—and so was the hope that he could be brought home safely.

By March, the volunteers had been observing Skidder's nightly patterns for two months. It had been ten months since he escaped. Fortunately, it had not been the harshest of winters, and spring was not far off. They knew something needed to be done *now*; winter had kept Skidder confined, but when spring came, he would be inclined to wander farther away from the ravines. The rescue learned from another rescue that there was a humane trap designed specifically for canines called a Collarum. One of the veterinarians working with Sandy and Briget had one and lent it to them.

Off they went on another trip to Michigan—but this time, they could stay for only one night. It was March 17, 2012. They set the Collarum directly on the path that Skidder traveled during the night. The retired couple's home provided warmth to the volunteers as the cameras sent them images of the terrain. They wondered whether Skidder would come by that night, and whether he would take the bait.

At a quarter after two in the morning, Skidder was detected on his usual path. He headed straight for the Collarum and immediately picked up the scent of the bait. He tentatively approached it. Then suddenly he turned and walked away, not to return that night. Sandy and Briget went home heartbroken.

Two weeks later, they tried again. It was April 1—April Fool's Day. This time, they would spend two nights watching and waiting. Again, the Collarum was set. The first night they didn't see Skidder at all, and they worried that something might have happened to him. By two thirty on the second night of their stay, they still hadn't seen Skidder. Their feelings of failure and sadness were all-consuming. But just a few minutes later, he appeared and approached the bait—and this time, he was not tentative.

Sandy and Briget sprinted down the beach, stumbling over rocks on the steep slopes. Skidder did not growl, bark, or whine—he just turned into a big marshmallow in their grasp. Not wanting to take the chance of him slipping away again, they carried a crate down to the Collarum. Skidder went into the crate willingly, and the women carried it up the steep bluff and loaded it into their car.

Skidder was captured on April 3, 2012, at 2:37 a.m. Briget and Sandy sent word out on the Internet: "We got him!"

You bet Sandy, Briget, and everyone involved believe Skidder was worth all the effort. They believe *all* the dogs are!

Unbelievably, after ten months of six-hundred-mile round trips and thousands of dollars spent on capture equipment, a tent, sleeping bags, cameras, and a custom-made pen—not to mention all the gas and oil for the vehicle—Skidder was finally safe. He had fleas and ticks, and his once-beautiful light-blond coat was filthy and matted, but he was alive and in fairly good shape. "Awesome!" or "Unbelievable!" was the general reaction from everyone who knew and followed the rescue's extraordinary efforts and what these two dog lovers did to save Skidder.

When you stop and think about it, this is not just the story of a remarkable dog and his survival; it is also the story of the incredible resolve of a group of volunteers in general, and two women in particular, who never gave up.

It is a story that describes five-star dog lovers at their best.

Part One

1995–2000

Dog Lovers and Dog Likers

ONE DAY, I WAS POISED OVER A GOLF BALL ON the putting green when a fellow golfer approached me and said, "Pat, how many dogs do you have?"

"Three," I answered.

"Three dogs? That's a lot. Why so many? Are you a dog lover?"

"No," I said. "For the record, I am a dog liker. I don't really need or want three dogs."

He looked at me and said, "Then why do you have three?"

"Are you married?" I asked him.

"Of course," was the reply.

I looked up at him. "Then why are you asking?"

There is a difference between a dog *lover* and a dog *liker*. I am a dog liker. My wife, Mary Ellen, is a dog lover. I am fond of dogs; she loves them to death. Dog lovers have a passion and love for every pooch they meet, and they bond with their own dogs in a way that dog likers can never begin to understand. To dog lovers, there is no such thing as a mean, nasty, or unfriendly dog. Such dogs are just the products of bad owners.

Dog lovers can't help themselves. Being a dog lover is in their souls; they were born that way. They could not change if they tried. Having a dog or another pet as a child helps bring out and expose this passion; these childhood experiences only reinforce their hidden devotion and prepare them for life as a dog lover. The five-star dog lovers gravitate to dog rescue. Here is a world made for them and just waiting for them and their passion.

Many people are born with a passion for something—the sick, the homeless, animals, and so forth—and they are motivated by the joy and pleasure they receive when they satisfy their passion. They do so by volunteering at neighborhood health clinics, soup kitchens, or animal shelters. They raise money to feed others and provide medical care. They pass out food and blankets to the homeless. Pass an animal shelter, and you will observe them walking and exercising dogs on the grounds. Others are inside comforting animals recovering from an illness. Many train family pets to be therapy dogs and take them to hospitals, nursing homes, and other places where they can interact with the patients or residents, providing comfort and solace.

These dog lovers possess a deep devotion to their passion and are willing to make a substantial commitment to pursue it. If their passion were associated with religion or politics, they would be called zealots.

Karl Menninger may have been thinking of dog lovers when he said that "the human being struggles with his environment and the hooks that catch him," and that "it is hard for a free fish to understand what is happening to a hooked one." The hooks of passion that dog lovers experience are deep and permanent. The depth of their passion and the struggles that accompany it are all that dog likers see, and they naturally misunderstand. It might be fair to say that it is hard for a dog liker to completely understand a dog lover.

All I know is that when it comes to dog lovers, the world is better off with them than without them. I also know that if all dog owners were at the very least dog likers, there would be little need for rescues.

Neiman Marcus

IT'S NOT THAT I'M UNCOMFORTABLE AROUND dogs or have not been exposed to them. I have two daughters, and when they were growing up we had Old English sheepdogs. Mary Ellen had a beagle as a child; later she gravitated to larger dogs.

When we met, she was recently divorced and living at home with her mother and a German shepherd named Neiman Marcus. I was in a post-divorce state as well. I asked her out to dinner, and when I arrived she was not quite ready. She brought me to her living room, told me to relax, and said she would not be long. I eased into an upholstered chair, and after she left, around the corner came Neiman, her German shepherd. Mary Ellen had mentioned him briefly in passing. He was a big shepherd with an aloof demeanor, a large head, and a black and tan coat. He definitely was not the warm, cuddly type of pet.

He walked slowly and quietly across the room, sat down in front of me, and just stared. His body was frozen, and his piercing, deep-brown eyes narrowed and bored holes in me as he concentrated on my face. He never moved a muscle, and I couldn't. For one of the few times in my life, I was terrified.

I considered bolting for the door but thought better of it, because there was no way around him. I reviewed my options and found there were none, so without raising my voice or sounding an alarm, I nonchalantly said, "Mary Ellen, could you come out here?"

"What's the matter?" she called out.

"Is your dog friendly?" I asked.

"Oh, Neiman. He won't bother you," she replied.

Somehow that did not alleviate the fear I felt at that time.

Finally, her makeup completed, Mary Ellen returned and smiled at the sight of the two of us staring at each other.

"Really, he is a gentle dog," she offered.

I got up slowly and navigated around Neiman, who remained fixed in the same spot. He just moved his head enough to continue to stare at me as I moved to the door. He never took his eyes off of me. As we left, he gave me a look that said, *If you don't bring her back, I will come looking for you.*

The evening went well, and we began dating. The only stipulation I put on the relationship was that she had to be ready to go whenever I arrived. There would be no more stare-downs between Neiman and me.

"I told you, Neiman is very gentle," she chided. "He won't hurt you."

"Do dogs get jealous?" I asked.

"Of course, some will show jealousy," she replied.

"In that case," I said, "how about you just be ready when I show up?"

Sometime later, Mary Ellen invited me over for dinner. Her mom was doing the cooking, and so before dinner, she and I relaxed on the sofa. As I said, Neiman was not a warm, cuddly type of dog. He would always position himself with his back to a wall where he could have a clear view of the room. When he saw us on the couch, he came over, got up on the sofa, and sat between us. He gave me one of his cold, steely stares that said, *Don't get too close to her.*

I sensed that the connection between Mary Ellen and Neiman was more than the usual one between owner and pet. I had never known a dog lover, however, so I did not recognize the symptoms. As our relationship progressed, we would chat, and I would listen to her talk about animals, dogs, and Neiman in particular. It was only then that I realized she was not just a dog owner; she was passionate about and devoted to animals. I didn't completely understand how she felt and what motivated her, but I did not view the trait as a hindrance or possible problem in our relationship.

We dated on and off for more than ten years. When Mary Ellen and I married in the early nineties, she owned a flat-coated retriever named Merlin, and he was coming with her. "Flat coats" are essentially golden retrievers with an all-black coat, but they are very high-strung. Think of a dog with attention deficit disorder.

Each and every time we came home, Merlin would greet us as if we had been separated for months or years. He would rush to the door, do wheelies, and promptly tear around the house. Ultimately he would present himself at our feet, and we would pet him and quiet him down.

Merlin was special, unlike any other dog Mary Ellen had had, and he was a dog lover's delight. She loved that dog dearly, but a few years into our marriage he died of cancer. The effect of his passing was dramatic. Mary Ellen agonized over his death and was left with a huge void in her life. Faced with her situation, dog likers like me would think *I never want to put myself through that again.* Dog lovers, on the other hand, despite their heavy hearts from having just experienced the torment of watching a beloved companion go through sickness and death, can't wait to begin anew.

And so, although I did not realize it then, I was about to be introduced to the world of dog rescue.

Morgan and Comet

MARY ELLEN WAS NOT THE SAME PERSON WITH-
out a dog in her life, so I encouraged her to begin the application
process with the local golden retriever rescue. After she jumped
through all the hoops and had her home visit, we were put on
the rescue's approved list and began waiting for the right dog to
come along. The call we anticipated came, and soon we were on
our way to a foster home. There, waiting for us, was a five-year-
old golden named Morgan.

Morgan was stoic, quiet, and shy. It was explained to us that
a teacher had called the rescue to report that a young student
was crying and saying that her mommy and daddy were not nice
to her dog anymore and kept him locked in the basement where
she could not play with him. The child also told the teacher that
her parents were going to give the dog away.

Rescue volunteers contacted the owners and heard a familiar story. The couple had purchased the puppy as a Christmas
present for their young daughter. Five years later, the dog was
doing what a young dog does—jumping, running around, and
generally getting under their feet and into things. They told the
rescue that he was just too much. They didn't want the bother of
caring for this young dog and were going to give him up. They
wanted him gone.

The rescue took the dog reluctantly, knowing a young child's heart would be broken. But the alternative was that the dog would be dropped off at the local shelter, and then who knew where he would end up? Many times in an overcrowded shelter, there is no room to place a new dog, and it ends up on the PTS list.

At the foster home, Mary Ellen got down on the floor and began to rub her hand over Morgan's head. She waited for him to get playful and carry on, as the previous owners had led everyone to believe he liked to do. But being left often in the basement, away from his family, had changed him. Now his head was slumped between his paws, and he stared up at her with sad eyes devoid of emotion. She continued stroking his head gently, and he continued to look at her with a blank gaze.

Meanwhile, the foster informed us of all she was able to learn about Morgan, which was not much. He had been with her for a month, and he spent most of his time lying in the den. He got along with everyone and wasn't a problem in any way; he was just quiet and withdrawn. He was no longer a rambunctious young dog, and he obviously missed his family.

It is amazing how loyal these animals are despite their harsh treatment. In some ways, they resemble the battered wife who stands by her man despite his abuse. Regardless of the ill treatment, dogs seldom resist; they will remain loyal to their owners until the end, patiently waiting for the day the abuse stops. But that day never comes.

The gentle rub and staring went on for quite some time until my wife looked up and said to the foster and the rescue owner, "I would like to have Morgan."

They asked if she was sure, and when she nodded, they left the room for a private conference. When they came back into the room, the rescue owner said, "When would you like to take him?"

Her answer was short and direct. "Now. I would like to take him home with me."

Morgan was the first in a long line of rescue dogs that we would adopt, and of all the dogs, he was the saddest and the most difficult to coax out of his shell. We brought him home, and suffice it to say he was far from an active and playful dog. Maybe he had been at one time, but not anymore. Having been taken from the only family he'd ever known, Morgan was confused. Worse, his spirit was broken.

At that time, we lived on a corner lot, and our living room had palladium windows that went almost to the floor. Opposite one of the windows was a school bus stop. Morgan would lie at that window all day, head between outstretched paws. We could cajole him into the kitchen for meals, but when he finished eating he would return to the window.

In the mornings, as the children gathered and waited for the bus, he would come alive. He would stand—ears up, nose to the windowpane, head moving back and forth, searching. He was trying to find the young girl who had been his companion. Finally, the bus would fill and leave. Only then would he lie back down.

Later in the afternoon, the hiss of the bus's brakes would catch his attention. Immediately he would put up his ears, and then his eyes would follow every child who left the bus. Just like the morning, it was only after all the children were gone that he would lie down.

That went on day after day.

We knew we had to do something to break this vigil and revitalize Morgan's spirit, and Mary Ellen had just the answer.

"He needs a playmate," she announced, and before long we were at another foster home, looking over a three-year-old male named Comet. Anything but shy and quiet, he was being dried off by the foster as we arrived. Apparently he had decided to take a dip in the family's spa.

While Morgan was short and stocky and sort of muscular-looking, Comet was tall and thin. Unwanted by his owners, he had been kept in a garage and neglected. When he came to the rescue, he was badly underweight and had no social skills. He jumped on Mary Ellen as we entered—not a way to impress a dog liker like me, but right up a dog lover's alley. I took one look at my wife and knew that Comet was coming home with us.

Dog likers usually have a one-dog limit. Dog lovers try to make room for every dog that needs them, if possible. They do have a reasonable limit, as opposed to hoarders—individuals with a pathological desire to take in and help every animal they find. The media is full of stories of hoarders who house huge numbers of animals, so many that it is impossible to feed and medically care for them. Usually the animals are removed by court order and turned over to rescue organizations. Hoarders need intense psychological therapy in order to recognize and break their destructive habit.

I must admit that my wife was right: the combination of summer recess and adding Comet to the family was just what Morgan needed to abandon his window ritual. Comet would put stuffed toys in Morgan's face and shake them, or drop tennis balls on his head—anything to get his attention. And if that didn't work, Comet would lift a paw and bop Morgan on the head. That would do it! Soon they would be playing, each dog on one end of a rope toy, tugging and pulling.

Shortly after Comet arrived, something curious happened. There was a laundry room separating our kitchen from the garage. When both my wife and I left the house, the dogs would lie in the laundry room and wait for us to return. In the laundry room, there was a door leading to a walk-in closet where we kept a large bag of dog food on the floor and supplies on the shelves. When we left, we were always very careful to check that the closet door was closed. For as long as we had only Morgan, there was never a problem. But after Comet arrived, we would return to find the closet door ajar. When we'd inspect the closet, however, nothing seemed to be amiss.

Initially we thought we were being careless, but after some time, we knew the problem was not us. Definitely something was going on. My wife and I could not solve the mystery, and it was driving both of us to madness. Determined to get some answers, we decided to set up our video camera on a tripod and turn it on the next time we left. When we returned from our next trip and found the closet door slightly open, we were anxious to view the tape.

Watching the video, we observed ourselves leaving and the door to the garage closing. Morgan and Comet rested quietly for a while, and then Comet got up and moved over to the closet door, which had a typical lever handle. Comet eased over, placed his nose under the brass lever, and brought it up, releasing the latch. Next he put his nose in the crack of the door and opened it enough for them to go in. Morgan, observing all this, got up and joined Comet. Together they looked around, inspecting the shelves, and then they approached and stared at the open twenty-five-pound bag of dog food. They looked at the food and then at each other, and with that they left and went back to resting on the floor. It was as if Comet had said to Morgan, "Don't worry; if they don't come back, at least we can eat."

Later, Comet would turn into an accomplished counter cruiser. He once ate half a loaf of bread, and on another occasion he polished off a stick of butter from the Thanksgiving table. One Christmas morning, he ate the better part of a holiday kuchen. Surprisingly, he never got sick as a result of his counter cruising, but we became more vigilant about where we placed our food. We also put a lock on the closet door in the laundry.

It was at about this time that Mary Ellen decided to join the rescue as a volunteer. By now, she was hooked on rescue, and she was about to begin a journey that would end with her becoming a five-star dog lover. She had already started down that path, to be sure, and there was no turning back. Her journey would be filled with joy and sadness and stories that would leave indelible marks on our hearts.

I didn't realize it then, but she was taking me with her. At the time, I thought I would probably learn a lot of surprising things about dogs, but what happened was that I learned an awful lot about human beings—and in the end, I found that I just might like dogs better.

The Dog Stealer

MY WIFE GRADUATED FROM COLLEGE WITH A degree in education, and her kindergarten students called her Teacher. Later she went back to school, got her nursing degree, and became a surgical nurse. In the operating room, the patients would call her Nurse. Some people in the neighborhood who did not know her name called her the Dog Lady. Among those who knew her, she was always referred to as a dog lover, but she was soon to acquire another name: the Dog Stealer.

At the time, she had just started volunteering for the rescue as a transporter. Basically, she would pick up dogs and drop them off at a veterinarian's office or a foster home—wherever they needed to go. The rescue had been called by the police department in a nearby suburb. A golden retriever had been turned in by a mail carrier who had found the dog wandering about on his route. The dog had no collar and no identification tags. He began to follow the mail carrier and after a time got into the mail truck. The carrier, who knew everyone on the route and had never seen this dog before, gave the dog some water and allowed him to stay in the truck for the remainder of the route. It was summertime, and people were out and about in their yards. As the carrier moved from street to street, he asked all the people he saw if they recognized the dog or knew the owner. No, no one recognized the dog.

Realizing that the dog was lost, the mail carrier finished his route and then dropped the dog off at the suburb's small police department. For three days, the policemen fed the dog and kept him in their office, expecting the owner to call or show up. In our city, owners are given three days to find and rightfully claim their dog—this is generally the law in most cities—and after that, a dog not claimed by its rightful owner is deemed abandoned, and anyone can claim it. So after three days, when no one called or came looking for the dog, the police called the rescue and said, "We have an abandoned golden retriever, and you can have it."

We lived in an adjacent suburb, and so the rescue asked my wife to pick up the dog and drop him off at a local veterinarian's office. After signing for the dog, she dropped him off with the vet and went on her way. When dogs are brought into the rescue, a veterinarian will usually examine the dog, check to see if it is chipped, and recommend medical treatment if necessary. Every dog brought into the rescue is vaccinated as needed and then spayed or neutered. So the veterinarian gave this dog the usual shots, neutered him, and removed a large growth, informing the rescue that the tumor was likely cancerous. From there, the dog went to a foster home, and you might think that the story was over, but it was just beginning.

About a week later, a lady called the police department looking for a golden retriever and claiming to be the owner. Checking their records, they gave the caller my wife's name and phone number. She then called Mary Ellen and demanded her dog back.

"How come you waited so long to look for him?" my wife asked her. "Why didn't he have a collar with identification tags?"

The caller offered no answers, and so Mary Ellen referred

her to the rescue's board of directors, who asked her for the name of her veterinarian and then told her they would get back to her. The veterinarian informed them that he had seen the dog on only one occasion. He had found the tumor, told the owner it was likely cancer, and recommended removal. The owner refused. He never saw the dog again. He had no record of the dog receiving the required shots or regular medical care.

By now the biopsy report on the tumor had confirmed that the growth was cancer. The board confronted the owner with the fact that the dog had for all practical purposes been neglected medically, and again they asked her why she'd waited more than a week to begin looking for him. The owner had no answers and again demanded that her dog be returned. Reluctantly, the board offered a compromise: if the owner promised to be more responsible and pay the vet bill for the shots, neuter, and tumor removal, they would return the dog to her. She refused their offer.

The board of the rescue, along with their attorney, pondered the situation. The attorney informed the rescue that legally the dog belonged to them. How could a dog be gone for over a week before his owner started looking for him? the board members wondered. Why no collar with tags? In addition, there was no indication that if they returned the dog to this owner, she would care for him any better than she had in the past. Clearly she was not a very responsible pet owner, and she'd given no indication that she was willing to change. The question that the board had to answer was, what was best for the dog? Given the owner's attitude, they told her they'd decided to keep the dog. But the storm was just brewing.

The owner had a relative, maybe a nephew, who had recently graduated from law school and just passed the bar exam. This newly licensed attorney assumed the job of getting the dog back, and the first thing he did was file an emergency motion with the local court to have the dog returned. It became apparent that he had not slept through the classes on mobilizing public support, because he next contacted each of the three major TV news outlets in the area.

One by one they brought their camera crews and reporters to the owner's living room. The owner would sit next to her granddaughter, who had a bow in her hair, bright eyes, and a sad expression on her face. The granddaughter would look directly into the TV camera and tell the reporter how much she and her grandmother missed Bo. Then the grandmother would look into the camera and describe how Mary Ellen Metro of Rocky River had stolen her dog and had him neutered and would not return him. She appeared to have been coached well and seemed to follow a script: call the dog by his name, state how much she loved him, mention as often as possible that Bo had been taken by Mary Ellen Metro of Rocky River, and then repeat how much she, and especially her granddaughter, missed Bo.

It was a great storyline: suburban housewife steals dog, has him neutered, and refuses to give him back, leaving the owner and granddaughter crushed with sadness. Over the next two days, each TV channel played its interview several times. Never once did any of the TV reporters contact Mary Ellen Metro or the board of the rescue for their side of the story. The media were not interested in the whole story.

Next, the owner's attorney got talk radio involved. Talk show hosts spent hours discussing the suburban dog stealer, Mary Ellen Metro of Rocky River. It was all over the local airwaves. The story was even picked up by Paul Harvey, the nationally syndicated talk-show host, who included it in one of his daily *The Rest of the Story* broadcasts. The board members of the rescue, the vets who worked with the rescue, and others who knew Mary Ellen and were aware there was a lot more to this story called in to the local radio station and tried to tell the hosts and their audience all the facts. The facts didn't sell airtime, however; a dog-stealing suburban housewife did.

One popular morning talk-radio show started a fund to raise money to pay Bo's medical bill. The following morning I was in my pajamas, about to take a shower, when I heard a commotion in front of our condo. Curious, I put on a robe and slippers and went out to investigate. Parked in front of the condo was a truck with a large antenna. The radio station was broadcasting live. I saw the radio host in his truck and heard him say, "I see someone coming out in his pajamas—I'll try to interview him." In addition to its live broadcast, the radio station had an employee walking around in a dog costume and carrying a bullhorn, chanting, "Give us Bo back! Give us Bo back!"

Hearing the commotion, our neighbors started coming out of their units. Some leaving for work stopped to ask what was going on. A crowd was gathering. I was waiting for TV trucks to pull up to get some footage; I envisioned myself being featured on the evening news in my robe and pajamas. Fortunately, the road in front of our condo was private property. Finally, the police made the radio host and his employees leave, and I was left to answer a lot of questions from our neighbors.

Later, as I worked my way through my office schedule, I learned that some of my patients had seen the story on TV and others had heard it discussed on talk radio, so they too peppered me with questions. Did my wife really steal that dog? Was that me in the pajamas? I fully expected that someday Mary Ellen and I would be dining out and someone would point at her and say, "That's her! She's the one that stole the dog." Clearly things were getting out of hand.

The rescue's board met again with their attorney. All this one-sided publicity was beginning to reflect negatively on Mary Ellen and the rescue. In addition, the judge had ordered that Bo be returned to his owner until she made a final decision, and she seemed to indicate that that was where Bo might ultimately remain. She had sent her bailiff to our house to check out our dogs and see if we were hiding Bo. The bailiff showed up and brought the owner, her attorney, and an assortment of the owner's relatives. (Fortunately there was no time for them to invite the media.) While Mary Ellen showed our dogs to the bailiff, one of the relatives—a young, tough-looking teen—made a fist and started pounding his open hand. He looked at me and said, "We're going to get both of you."

I went to the local police station and related the threat but did not file a formal report. I got the usual admonition that if he returned or came on our property or issued any more threats, I should contact them. Somehow that did not seem very reassuring.

All this time, Mary Ellen had been the focus of the media attention and was being portrayed as totally responsible for the stolen dog. What was lost was the fact that she'd become involved because she was acting as a transport volunteer for a rescue organization. At first we'd found humor in the thought of Mary Ellen being portrayed as a suburban dog stealer, but now the situation was getting ugly, and it needed to end. It wasn't so much all the negative attention as the fact that we were concerned for our safety.

While the rescue had the law on its side, the dog's owner and her attorney appeared to have the judge's sympathy. With no end in sight, this battle could drag on a long time and only get worse. Ultimately this judge might order Bo returned to his owner for the same reason well-meaning judges return children to homes where they've been abused and neglected.

And so the board made a painful but practical decision: the radio station would pay the veterinarian's bill, and Bo would go back to his former home. It was a sad ending for all the rescue volunteers, because they felt it was a bad ending for Bo and they had let him down. The rescue tried numerous times to get some follow-up information on Bo but was unsuccessful.

Walking away was a practical decision but a difficult one to accept. Not all rescues end up with happy endings. Mary Ellen was learning that in the rescue business, you take the good with the bad.

Carrie

THE EXPERIENCE WITH BO CERTAINLY WOULD have discouraged a dog liker, but being the dog lover that she was, Mary Ellen only became more involved. She was advancing as a dog lover, having moved up from three stars to four. Yes, she was working full-time, but we had no children to care for, and it was her decision to devote her spare time to dog rescue.

At the urging of Sandy and April, two of the rescue's board members, Mary Ellen expanded her participation and started doing home visits as well as intake and adoptions along with her transport duties. She would make rescue calls on her lunch break at the hospital, and after dinner she would sit on the den floor and make additional calls while grooming our dogs.

Like Mary Ellen, Sandy was a registered nurse, and like April, she had been in the rescue business for a long time. Together Sandy and April would teach Mary Ellen everything they knew, but they could not prepare her for her experience with Carrie, a dog she would soon bring into the rescue.

Shortly after the Bo experience, Mary Ellen was working with a single woman in her thirties who had contacted the rescue wanting to relinquish her older golden. The dog was a female more than ten years old, and her name was Carrie. The woman had gotten Carrie when she was a puppy. Carrie had bright eyes, a long flowing coat, and a delightful personality. Her playful days were limited now, but she loved to cuddle. Her owner was a professional who traveled occasionally, and Carrie was always there waiting for her when she returned at the end of a workday or business trip. But now there was a new man in the owner's life, and he did not like dogs, so Carrie had to go. Carrie had comforted her on quiet evenings and lonely weekends, but now her new man would fill that job, and Carrie wasn't needed anymore.

The intake forms were all signed, and Mary Ellen and I arranged to meet the woman early one morning in a designated mall parking lot. We described our SUV and said we would be there with the hatchback open. She arrived and parked next to us. I observed her as she exited her car. She was tall and attractive with short brunette hair and was smartly dressed in a sweater and slacks. She had an air of confidence about her, and I guessed she had a management position.

We were standing alongside our vehicle when she got out of her car, walked up to Mary Ellen, and handed her Carrie's water bowl and one of her stuffed toys. When she went back to fetch Carrie, I was not sure what to expect next. I thought about how I'd feel giving up a dog I'd raised from a puppy and lived with for more than ten years, and I was prepared for an emotional scene. But what happened next stunned both Mary Ellen and me, and we would never forget it. The young woman simply took Carrie out of the car, walked her over to us, and handed the leash to Mary Ellen. She flashed a polished smile and said, "It was nice meeting you." Then she got into her car and drove off. No pat on Carrie's head with a "You be a good girl" No hug or kiss good-bye.

Mary Ellen and I just stood there in disbelief. Carrie had given her owner more than ten good years, and it meant nothing to this heartless woman. We'd never witnessed anything so callous or cold.

When the woman got into her car, Carrie started making whimpering sounds and pulling on the leash. She wanted to be with the person who'd been in her life since she was a puppy. Finally, as the car moved farther and farther away, Carrie began to bark, but the woman was gone. I couldn't stop myself. I yelled, "I hope you're happy, you miserable SOB!" I knew she couldn't hear me, but I yelled it anyway, and letting it out made me feel better. It was early in the morning, and the only people around were an older couple out for a stroll. They witnessed the exchange and my outburst, and they gave me a big smile as they walked by.

We put Carrie in our SUV. I drove while Mary Ellen sat in the back and tried to comfort the sad, confused dog. Not surprisingly, the woman who'd given her up never once called to ask where Carrie was or how she was doing. Usually when owners relinquish their dogs, they have the option to call and inquire about their former pets. The bond between pet and owner is not easily severed, and former owners often want to know about their dogs' foster and permanent homes and how their dogs are adjusting. But we never heard from Carrie's owner again.

Dog lovers simply cannot understand the mind-set of owners like that one, who walked away from a pet she'd had for years. Was the owner incapable of bonding? Did she lack love and compassion? Certainly some individuals do not have the ability to form bonds with other humans, so it's not a stretch to suggest that they lack whatever is necessary to bond with a nonhuman. In the same way, many people walk away from a marriage after years of living in a close, bonded relationship and never look back.

But dog lovers see walking away from an adult who is capable of taking care of himself or herself very differently from leaving a pet. To dog lovers, walking away from a pet is akin to abandoning a child. And when children are abandoned, it is usually due to alcohol, drugs, or other problems, not simply because their parents don't want them anymore. The topic of owners walking away from their pets after sharing years together is often discussed among dog lovers, and no one seems to be able to provide a satisfactory answer. Giving a dog up may demonstrate that you are uncaring, but opening a car door and letting a pet out to fend for itself borders on cruel. How do you abandon a pet in that manner? That is something both dog lovers and dog likers find offensive.

So why do owners who profess love for their dogs give them up? These same owners will also say that they love their new car or house. The love they profess is a love that comes from ownership. In time, the newness wears off and the possession is no longer attractive to them, and so they get rid of it. Over the years, Mary Ellen would meet many dog owners who fit into this category.

Placing older dogs is not easy. Most adopters want younger dogs that presumably will be with them longer. It took a little time, but Mary Ellen found the perfect adopters for Carrie—a retired couple who qualified as dog lovers. They opened their hearts to Carrie and provided her with the love and comfort she needed as well as the life she deserved.

Allie

THERE WAS A VETERINARIAN WITH A CLINIC near the hospital where Mary Ellen worked. His name was Boris, and Mary Ellen was in and out so often with rescue dogs that she became a regular around his office.

Boris would go to a pet store in a nearby shopping mall to give new puppies their necessary vaccines. On one visit, the owner of the store showed him a newly arrived puppy that appeared to be sick. Boris examined the puppy and said that she probably had parvo, a highly contagious disease that is often fatal. The owner wanted to protect the other dogs in the store, so he asked Boris to take the puppy with him and put her to sleep.

When Boris returned to his clinic with the puppy, Mary Ellen happened to be there. When she saw the puppy and heard the story, she asked him, "Can that puppy be saved?"

"Parvo in puppies is almost always fatal," Boris replied. "Even if they survive, they are often left weak and require a lot of special care. Also, finding someone to adopt them can be a problem."

"If you save her, I will find a good home for her," Mary Ellen told him.

"She will need a lot of prayers," Boris offered.

"I will do the praying if you do the rest," she retorted.

With that, Boris started treatment. Each day after her work as a surgical nurse, Mary Ellen would stop by his clinic and don the mask and gown she had brought with her from the hospital.

By now, the puppy had a name: Allie. Because parvo is so contagious, Allie had to be separated from the other dogs in Boris's kennel. Each day when Mary Ellen would arrive, she would find Allie off in a corner on a blanket, curled up and sleeping. Cradling the little ball of fur in her arms for maybe an hour, Mary Ellen would rock and gently stroke and pet her. Allie was so ill that she would sleep the entire time. This went on for weeks.

Then Mary Ellen began to notice subtle changes—a feeble wave of the tail or a light kiss on Mary Ellen's mask. They were sure signs that Allie was getting better.

Gradually, the combination of Boris's medical care and Mary Ellen's nursing and prayers worked. Allie continued to improve, and in time she experienced full recovery, which is unusual for parvo puppies. She was never a robust dog, as the parvo left her susceptible to illness, but she was able to play and take her walks. She couldn't participate in strenuous activity, but otherwise she was not very different from most other pets.

Allie was placed in a forever home with a volunteer who'd been waiting for a special dog with a challenge. The new owner's name was Kim, and she helped Allie live a full life for almost fifteen years.

Puppy Pilot

AS ANY BREEDER WILL TELL YOU, NOT ALL LIT-
ters produce puppies that look like they belong on the cover of a
dog magazine. Quite often, one or more puppies in a litter will be
born with a minor or serious defect. They may be deaf, blind, or
lame, or have skeletal or medical issues, such as epilepsy. These
puppies are always passed over in the selection process, and
breeders are left with the choice of euthanizing them or turning
them over to a rescue.

Such dogs are a challenge to rescue organizations, because it
takes more than empathy for a prospective owner to adopt a dog
that will require a lifetime of special care and devotion. These
dogs sometimes spend a long time in foster care before a suitable
and willing owner can be found. Often, however, these adoptions
make the most satisfying stories.

One day a breeder contacted the rescue to say that one of the
puppies in her latest litter—a male now about two months old—
had been born blind. As long as he had his littermates to follow,
he did fine navigating her house. But one by one they'd been
sold off, and now he was alone, struggling to fend for himself
when the owner was gone. She could not sell him, and she could
not keep him. She was going to have him put to sleep unless the
rescue wanted him.

The rescue took the puppy. He had a beautiful reddish coat, but his eyes told you he could not see. The rescue's veterinarian examined him and found him healthy, and then he said, "What are your plans for this puppy?"

In truth, there was no plan. They simply decided to keep him and hope for the best.

The veterinarian then said, "I suggest you take this puppy to an eye specialist." He recommended a veterinary ophthalmologist.

When Mary Ellen and the puppy arrived for their appointment with the eye specialist, the veterinary technician who took them back to the examination room was very interested in the puppy, asking all sorts of questions about the breeder and wanting any other information Mary Ellen could share. The technician thought the puppy was adorable, and she spent some time telling Mary Ellen that puppies can be trained to live with a handicap and will overcome it much more easily than dogs that go blind after having had normal eyesight.

"The right person could do a lot with this puppy," she added.

Mary Ellen listened carefully as the vet tech gave her tips for handling blind dogs. At the same time, Mary Ellen could not help but notice how well the puppy responded to the technician.

Finally the veterinary specialist entered the room. He examined the little guy, confirmed that the blindness was permanent, and said, "I wish I could keep him here for you, but we have no room." He paused for a moment before adding, "This puppy is otherwise healthy; it would be a shame to euthanize him."

As the veterinary technician left the examining room, she said, "Don't you give up on that puppy. It is amazing how well they will acclimate to their handicap. Take your time and find the right home for him."

Mary Ellen thanked her, and as she drove away, she mulled over the sage advice, wondering where she could find the right home for a puppy with such a severe handicap. She dropped the

puppy off at a foster home, and for the next few days she agonized over what to do with him, because she did not have a list
titled "Adopters Looking for Puppies with a Handicap."

Who would want a blind dog? she asked herself. She had been
around long enough to know the answer: *No one.*

Just then, the phone rang. It was the veterinary technician
from the ophthalmologist's office. "Have you found a home for
the blind puppy?" she asked.

"Not yet, but we are working on it," was the answer.

"Well," the vet tech said, "I would like to take him."

"Are you sure?" Mary Ellen asked in disbelief.

"Oh yes, definitely. I have plans for him," the vet tech replied.

She sure did have plans for that puppy! The veterinary technician's name was Allison, and what she did next was absolutely
remarkable. Allison had a mixed breed named Jessie at home,
and the blind puppy followed Jessie everywhere. They would
play, eat, and nap together. In her spare time, Allison was an avid
bicyclist, so she added a sidecar to her bike, placed the puppy
inside, and put goggles over his eyes. He looked like the Red
Baron, and so she named the puppy Pilot. Off they would go, with
a big smile on Pilot's face and the wind blowing his ears back.

That would have been a good ending, but there is more to
the story, as Allison was also into dog agility, big-time. First
she taught Pilot to rely on and respond to her voice, so that in
time he focused on her voice for everything and understood
her commands. Next she began agility training using her voice
and a small bell. In agility, dogs are placed in a ring where ob-
stacles like bars, hoops, tubes, and small ponds are set up in a
prescribed manner. Through endless hours of training, Allison
taught Pilot the course. At first she walked him through it slowly.
If he missed a bar or a hoop or ended up walking through a pond,
she would stop and repeat the command.

Once he mastered that, she moved on to the next phase of

training: when he was approaching an obstacle, she would ring the bell and shout a command—"Jump!" or "Run!"—and off he would go, up and over the bar or straight through the tube.

Ultimately, with Allison's coaching, he never missed. He became so accomplished that she soon had him tearing around the ring to the delight and amazement of everyone watching. Although he did not enter competitions, he was always the star attraction. Watching him perform, people would shake their heads in disbelief. "Really—is the dog *totally* blind?" they would ask.

My Name Is Amelia

EARLY ONE MORNING, AN EMPLOYEE OF A LOCAL animal shelter parked her car, approached the shelter door, and noticed a golden retriever tied to a post outside. Attached to the dog was a note: "My name is Amelia and I am three years old. I was hit by a car when I was a puppy and lost my leg. Please find me a good home."

The worker looked, and sure enough, Amelia was missing a front leg. She was a darling golden retriever, and the shelter workers found her to be a sweet, gentle, kind, and loving dog. Bright-eyed with a shimmering, pale-gold coat, she moved well; the loss of her front leg did not seem to hinder her in any way. Before long, everyone at the shelter loved her, and they thought that with her temperament, she should be easy to adopt out. Surely someone looking for a pet would come along and fall in love with this adorable golden girl.

The shelter tried and tried but was unable to find anyone interested in Amelia. No one saw the sweet, gentle temperament; all they saw was a missing leg. In desperation, the shelter called rescue.

After Mary Ellen took Amelia home, she began calling everyone on the foster and adopter lists and found the same sense of reluctance faced by the shelter. The fact that the dog had only three legs created some block in the minds of fosters and pro-spective adopters, and she could not get them to move beyond it and see Amelia any other way. She asked them to consider the dog's temperament and personality, but no coaxing or pleading worked. She could not find anyone to take Amelia.

This is not unusual. Placing handicapped dogs is extremely difficult. They require a level of time, care, and devotion that goes beyond the normal owner-pet relationship. Handicapped dogs cannot do many of the typical owner–pet activities; conse-quently, there is a hesitation to adopt these dogs. Most owners want a dog with which they can share life activities. They hes-itate to take a dog that is limited in its activities and requires constant care and attention. However, when the right owners are found for handicapped dogs, they can form the strongest owner–pet bonds imaginable, producing some of the most heartening success stories.

Finally a woman on the foster list called Mary Ellen back, saying she would give Amelia a try. She had a greyhound and a large, fenced-in yard where he could run. Mary Ellen won-dered what a greyhound and a three-legged golden retriever would find in common. How would they play? It didn't sound too encouraging, but she had no other offers; no one else was even interested.

"I will try her," the foster said when she came to pick Amelia up, "but if it doesn't work out, you need to promise to come get her. I have some reservations, but I will see how it goes and get back to you."

A couple of days later, the foster called and asked, "Have you found a home for Amelia?"

Expecting the worst, Mary Ellen responded, "Well, not yet. Do you want to return her?"

"Heavens no—I want to keep her! I can't begin to tell you

what a joy Amelia is and how much she has done for my greyhound. They have become inseparable. I just couldn't give her back."

Amelia spent the rest of her days chasing and being chased around the yard. It was a match made in heaven. Her owner's name was added to a different list. The list was named "Foster Failures," and the owners on it were proud to refer to themselves by that title.

Jetta

THE VOLUNTEERS AT THE RESCUE WOULD MEET with its board of directors on a regular basis, gathering at a coffee shop to assign various tasks and discuss the business of the rescue. Stories were also exchanged. At one meeting, two new volunteers heard the story of a dog that was being abused but whose owner would not give it up. They asked the board what could be done in these situations.

"Nothing," they were told. "We do not steal dogs or do anything unlawful. If we did, we would be out of business."

The answer bothered them. "How can you just ignore the situation?" one of them asked. "Aren't we in the rescue business?"

On the way out of the meeting, one of the older, experienced volunteers took the newbies aside and said, "Sometimes you do what you have to do, and you hope and pray that the owner doesn't get another dog and start all over again."

Many calls that come into rescues are from neighbors wanting to report a dog that is being abused or neglected. Their stories are similar: They observe the abuse firsthand, sometimes on a daily basis, and it disturbs them. They try talking to the owner but to no avail. Next they notify county animal protective services, and someone from that agency comes out and talks to the owner. The owner is told that the dog needs some kind of shelter, that it needs food and water, and that it needs medical care, including the vaccines required by the county, such as rabies. The county gives the owner a warning, and the owner ignores the citation. The abuse and neglect continue.

Most often, the authorities do not bother to return and check on owner compliance. In the few instances when they do return for a follow-up visit, nothing has been done, and so they simply issue another citation and leave. When is the last time you heard about an animal services agency removing a dog from an owner because of abuse and neglect? It does not happen often enough.

As a last resort, the neighbors call an animal shelter or rescue to describe the deplorable conditions and beg someone to help. One such neighbor called the rescue where Mary Ellen was a volunteer, wanting to discuss an older woman who lived nearby and owned a young female golden. The woman lived alone and never brought the dog into her house. She would put out food and water but paid no attention to the dog—no walks, no playing in the yard, no visits to the veterinarian, nothing. The woman's neighbors could not understand why she kept the dog.

In the summer, the dog was out in the blistering sun with no shade, and so they called animal services, who cited the owner for no vet care and lack of shelter. All the owner did was lean a piece of plywood against her house for shade. The compliance officer paid a rare return visit, saw the plywood, and left, never checking to see if the dog was up to date on her shots. Case closed!

So one Friday night, in response to the neighbor's call, two perky and energetic volunteers from the rescue got in their car and headed to the owner's house. They left their suburb and headed into the city, following the directions they'd been given. After a while, they moved from the outer city to the inner city, and they began to feel uncomfortable and concerned. They sensed it was not safe for two young women to be wandering these streets. As they drove, they passed junk and scrap-metal yards, with abandoned cars scattered here and there. They saw men huddled in doorways. This was a drug-infested area, and they were alarmed and about to turn back when they saw the name of the street they were searching for.

They turned onto the residential street and drove slowly, looking for the address they had been given. The street consisted of small, rundown bungalows situated close together, with small yards. Finding the right address, they pulled up and parked. It was late January in northern Ohio, and an arctic wind with snow was blowing off Lake Erie. During the day, the temperature had hovered around freezing, but now, late in the evening, it had dropped into single digits.

The volunteers approached the darkened house, and no one responded to their knocks or ringing of the doorbell. On the side of the house they found the young golden wedged between the house and the plywood. Nearby were two bowls, one with water and another with some kibble, both frozen solid. During the day, the dog had been lying in a pool of water. When she got up to greet the volunteers, she was shivering; the water was now a frozen pancake attached to her side. While one volunteer attended to the dog, the other went to an adjacent house. There an elderly couple told her the owner had left the city to visit friends, as she often did, and would not be back until Monday or Tuesday.

"Is someone looking after the dog?" the volunteer asked.

"No," the elderly woman answered. "She never bothers to have someone care for her dog when she leaves town."

Although these were not the neighbors who had called the golden rescue, they told the volunteers the entire neighborhood would be pleased if someone found the dog a new home.

The volunteer went back to her partner and shared what she had learned. A winter storm was coming, and the weather was predicted to worsen, with temperatures dropping below zero. They both looked at the shivering dog and pondered what would happen if they left her; they wondered if she would make it through the weekend without freezing to death. But they were in the business of dog rescue, not dog theft. They decided they'd take the dog home and shelter her until the owner came back, and then they would return her.

They shook off the snow and the frozen pancake from the dog's coat, wrapped her in a blanket, and put her in their car. Before they drove away, they left a phone number with the neighbor and asked her to notify them when the owner returned from her out-of-town visit. The neighbor promised to call them and then sent them off by saying, "Be careful—this is not the safest area for you to be driving around."

They didn't know the dog's name, so on the way home, as they were weaving their way through traffic following a Volkswagen, they decided to name her Jetta.

A few days later, as promised, the neighbor called and reported that the owner was back. When some neighbors had asked the owner what had happened to her dog, she told them, "I think she ran away."

"Have you called to see if anyone has turned her in anywhere?" they asked her. "Do you want us to look for her?"

"No," she said. "I am not going to bother. I will be moving out of the city soon, and I didn't plan to take her with me anyway."

The rescue volunteers waited a few weeks, and sure enough, the owner did just as she said. She moved to another city, never having placed a single call to report her dog missing or to see if the dog had been turned in anywhere—not to the police, not to the animal shelters, and not to any other agency.

If the owner didn't want the dog, well then, the volunteers knew just where the dog would be welcome. On the list of approved adopters was a recently divorced mom with a young daughter. It was a perfect match and a happy ending. Every

Christmas, these two volunteers would get a card with a picture of the mom and daughter with Jetta sitting between them wearing a big warm smile and a red bow. In rescue circles, Jetta's saviors were known as Thelma and Louise.

Get Out of Here
before I Shoot You

A YOUNG, ENTHUSIASTIC VOLUNTEER NAMED Chris was answering the hotline when a caller told her about a neighbor with a young golden puppy. The owner was a retiree who lived alone. He drank all day and too much. The dog was chained to a tree in the front yard, and being a puppy, he barked at everyone passing on the sidewalk. The dog craved attention, but the owner just ignored him. If he continued to bark or cry at night, the drunken owner would come out and yell at the dog to shut up. If this did not work, he would hit the puppy with a club.

On a recent occasion, he hit the dog so hard he broke the dog's front leg. He never bothered taking the dog to a veterinarian, and as a result, the lower part of the leg stuck out sideways at an odd angle. The neighbors contacted animal services, but the owner had connections in city hall. To make matters worse, in addition to his drinking problem, he had a volatile temper and a gun. Everyone in the neighborhood was afraid of him. No one was going to come out and cite this owner for anything.

Hearing this, the peppy young volunteer decided to drive over to confront the owner. A recent college graduate with a degree in psychology, Chris thought she was prepared to handle any type of situation. She was going to put all those psychology courses to good use. Wearing white shorts and a bright T-shirt with the words Golden Retriever Rescue across the front, her long blond hair pulled back into a ponytail and her sunglasses perched on top of her head, she thought she had come prepared. She would be polite to the retiree and offer to find a new home for his puppy, or even buy the dog if necessary.

After arriving at the house, Chris walked up the front steps, put a big smile on her face, and knocked on the screened door. A large man in a sweaty undershirt showed up. He looked down at the pretty, petite volunteer and slurred, "Whataya want?"

"Hello, sir. I would like to talk to you about your dog," she replied. But before she could say any more, he looked at her through bloodshot eyes and said, "Get out of here. And if you ever come back, I'll shoot you."

She stood there, stunned.

"Get off my property before I shoot you right now!" he bellowed.

Shaking, she backed down the steps, glanced over at the barking puppy, got into her car, and left.

That night, Chris shared the story with her boyfriend, Mark. She was still distraught and shaken from her encounter with the drunken owner and could not get the puppy out of her mind. Mark was just back from two tours with the army in Iraq. He had seen a lot of death and misery there and thought he was hardened to it all, but as Chris related the details of her earlier visit, he was deeply moved and disturbed. This story bothered him. He started thinking of the barking puppy with the crooked leg.

"I want you to take me there tomorrow," he said.

"I don't know if that is a good idea," Chris replied. "This owner is a crazy, dangerous drunk. He also has a gun. I'm afraid something will happen."

Mark ended the conversation by saying, "Let me handle everything."

The following evening, Chris and Mark drove to the drunken owner's neighborhood, parked their car, and took a walk past the house. No golden retriever T-shirt this time—both of them wore sloppy clothes with baseball caps. They paused to pet the puppy, and he started to bark. With that, a light came on in the house. Chris began to panic, remembering her earlier encounter with the owner, but Mark was prepared and calmed her down. He reached into his pocket, pulled out some pieces of hot dog, and dropped them on the ground. The puppy immediately began to search for and devour them, the barking stopped, and the light went out. By the time the puppy had searched out all the pieces of hot dog, Chris and Mark had left.

Two or three times a week through the summer, they visited the puppy and repeated the hot dog trick to keep him from barking. Sometimes they brought pieces of cooked liver; that quickly became the puppy's favorite treat. They were careful. The last thing they wanted to do was deal with this drunken owner who had a gun, and so they avoided a confrontation. By the end of the summer and after many visits, the puppy recognized them and would allow them to approach and feed him without so much as a cry or a whine. Instead of barking, he greeted them by wagging his tail frantically, anticipating whatever treat they brought.

Then one night, Mark walked up to the puppy alone. Chris was sitting in the car nearby with the motor running. While the puppy was munching on the pieces of hot dog and liver, Mark watched the house for activity. Seeing and hearing none, he reached into his pocket, pulled out a pair of metal cutters, and snipped the chain attached to the puppy's collar. He motioned to Chris, who slowly moved the car, lights off, along the curb toward the house. Mark slipped a finger under the puppy's collar and slowly started walking him to the curb. The puppy, absorbed with munching the morsels of meat Mark held in his hand, moved along with him. Chris pulled up, Mark opened the back door and climbed into the backseat with the puppy, and they quietly drove off.

The mission was pulled off with a precision that would make any army ranger proud. They didn't tell the rescue what they had done for fear that they would be told to return the puppy. They both knew that was something they absolutely could not do. Sometimes you just do what you have to do.

They were very close to Chris's veterinarian, and so they confided in her, telling her the entire story of what had transpired. She thought it over and finally agreed to break and reset the deformed leg. The surgery was a success, but the veterinarian had better news: the puppy was not chipped.

Many owners have a microchip inserted between their dogs' shoulder blades. Microchips carry an owner's address and phone number. Should the dog be lost or stolen and taken to a veterinarian for medical care, the original owner's name would appear on the screen, and the veterinarian would not release the dog until the owner listed on the chip was contacted and any discrepancy cleared up.

Veterinarians scan for chips as a matter of routine on a dog's initial visit. Likewise, checking for a chip is the first thing most animal welfare agencies, including rescues, do when they take in a dog. Microchips are a reliable way to recover a dog that may have wandered off its property and gotten lost; many dogs are returned to their owners in this manner.

Chris and Mark, who lived on the other side of the city from the drunken retiree, were concerned that he would simply find a new puppy to abuse. Often they would make the trip across town to drive by the house, and to their relief, all they ever saw was the chain hanging from the tree. No dog was ever attached.

Lucky, as they named the puppy, went to a new home, and

Chris quietly continued to volunteer with the rescue. Her experience with Lucky and his drunken owner matured her. In time, she realized that all her psychology courses could not prepare her for everything she would face in the world of dog rescue. Perhaps that is one of the graduate courses. Many years passed before she shared this story.

Part Two

2000–2015

A New Beginning

AT THE TURN OF THE CENTURY, I SOLD MY PRAC-
tice and retired. Up until then, we'd had a seasonal home in
Naples, Florida, and after a few years of driving back and forth
from Ohio, we began considering moving to Naples permanently. At that time we had three goldens, and the two-day drive
from Ohio to Florida was proving to be too much of a hassle. It
reminded me of a John Candy vacation movie, with our cargo
camper perched on the top of our SUV. Inside, the windows were
covered with nose smears known as "dog art," and I had traded
my usual Gucci loafers and Polo button-down for Nike sneakers
and a warm-up suit.

During the drive, we had to take our daytime meals in the
car; it was too hot to leave the dogs in the car, so going into a
restaurant and having a sit-down lunch was out of the question.
Usually we managed with food from McDonald's or another
fast-food chain. Try eating french fries with three dogs in the
backseat: either you share or they join you in the front seat. That
might have been amusing and fun for a dog lover, but as a dog
liker, I found that two days of this was about all I could handle.

Driving to Florida meant going only halfway the first day
and staying overnight in South Carolina after finding a motel
that allowed dogs, which was difficult back then. On our first

trip, we found a Holiday Inn that allowed dogs, but it must have been owned by a dog liker, because it had a one-dog limit. We checked in and brought our three dogs into the room one at a time through a side entrance, hoping no one would notice. We were assigned a room near an exit door at the back of the motel. Behind the motel there was a large grassy area that owners could use to exercise their dogs. The motel routinely assigned guests with dogs a room at the rear of the motel so the owners could easily avail themselves of this feature and any in-and-out traffic or barking would not disturb the nondog guests.

Because of the one-dog limit, Mary Ellen planned to walk the dogs one at a time. In the morning, they were always up early, and the first thing that had to be done was to take them out to relieve themselves, and so she got up about six. But when she attempted to leave with one dog, one of the other two, the barker, began carrying on to the point that he was going to wake everyone in the adjacent rooms. So she quieted the barker down and decided to take him with her, taking her chances with two dogs on the first trip. Sure enough, the grassy area was empty; no one was up to notice her and her two dogs. But when she returned to the building, she found the exit door locked. Then she noticed a little sign that read, "Between the Hours of 11:00 p.m. and 7:00 a.m., Please Use Front Entrance."

"Oh, great. Now what?" she murmured to herself. The door would not open, and she had no way back into the motel. Since it was so early, there was no one around to open the door from the inside; she could be there a long time waiting for someone to show up. Left with no choice, she walked both doggies around the motel to the front entrance and entered through the front door, only to find the night clerk at the desk, huddled over coffee with a sheriff's deputy. She quickly walked past them— and then, remembering it was South Carolina, she smiled and tried her best to sound a bit southern when she said, "Morning, gentlemen."

The clerk and the deputy were leaning in toward each other, deep in conversation. Neither looked up, but the deputy tipped his hat. "Morning, ma'am," they murmured as they continued sipping their coffee and chatting, never noticing that the lady passing them had two leashes and two dogs.

Eventually, we found that we were spending more time in Florida and less in Ohio, and so the decision to move to Florida permanently came easily for me. If you were not working, the time between November and April in northern Ohio was problematic. Gray skies and cold, windy days—not to mention the winter snow—curtailed any outdoor activities. Fishing and golf were out of the question. In Florida, however, you could pursue these activities all year round.

Mary Ellen was still working at the hospital and donating her spare time to rescue work. Moving to Florida permanently meant that she would most likely have to retire from her nursing career. But the hardest part would be giving up the rescue work with her partners, Sandy and April, and leaving all the dogs she had rescued, as well as the many dog-lover friends she'd made in and out of the rescue. She had forged a close bond with Sandy and April while volunteering with GRIN, which rescued between one hundred and two hundred dogs a year. It was a busy rescue that required a lot of coordinated work. The volunteers never knew what the next day would bring; sometimes multiple dogs would come in at the same time, and then everyone would spring into action.

Mary Ellen wondered what she would do with all her time. Moving meant she'd have to find new acquaintances and forge new friendships. And what about rescue, which was such an important part of her life? She was very reluctant to make this life-changing move.

As for me, after thirty-five-plus years of sixty-hour work-weeks and being on call to the emergency room twenty-four hours a day, I was more than ready to retire. I'd spent my hospital residency years in Cincinnati, and when I finished in the midsixties, I returned to northern Ohio to start a private practice in oral/maxillofacial surgery. I also spent time teaching residents at University Hospital, which was associated with Case Western Reserve University Medical School and was its teaching hospital.

In addition to routine office surgeries, much of my time over the years was spent in the hospital doing major facial-bone reconstruction to correct congenital deformities. Many of my other surgeries repaired traumatic injuries or reconstructed a face after tumor removal. I also spent many nights putting a motorcyclist's face back together after his Harley hit a car that was coming from the opposite direction and suddenly turned left in front of him. The bike would hit the turning car at the right front fender, and the rider would be projected over the hood and become a human missile, bouncing his face off the pavement several times.

Before seat belts and shoulder harnesses were required, drivers and passengers in automobiles had nothing to restrain them, and so every rear-end crash ended up with the driver's face smashed into the steering wheel and the passenger's face plastered against the windshield. I can be very critical of government overreach, but mandatory seat restraints for drivers and passengers have not only saved lives but also prevented countless injuries. In those days before mandatory seat restraints, I would be called to the emergency room two or three times a week, every week. Many of the injuries were minor, but quite often they were serious.

I spent a lot of time in emergency rooms over the years, and after a night of repairing a broken face, I'd catch a couple of hours' sleep and then be back in the office at eight, facing a full schedule of patients. These surgeries were grueling, and the routine was draining and began taking its toll. I was looking forward to lazy days filled with golf, fishing, and just relaxing. It was called "retirement," and I was ready for it. However, that was not what Mary Ellen was thinking; relaxing in retirement never crossed her mind. We seemed to be at an impasse.

One evening we sat down and talked things out. She agreed to try living in Florida permanently, but in return I had to promise to help her find a rescue to work with—or start her own rescue from scratch.

Before long, we'd moved into our seasonal home and become permanent Florida residents. I'd joined a golf club and easily found friends there, and I quickly settled into a new routine. Mary Ellen started out helping a rescue from the east coast of Florida as their representative in the Naples area, but she had other ideas. She kept talking about starting her own golden retriever rescue, as there wasn't one based in Naples. In our discussions, I would point out that starting a rescue from scratch would be a huge undertaking, like starting a business. First we'd need IRS approval and a board of directors. Then we'd need insurance and volunteers, veterinarians who would discount their services, a telephone hotline, and a website—as well as donations to pay for it all. And that was just for starters.

Mary Ellen was not deterred by the enormity of starting a dog rescue from scratch. She only became more determined to go forward.

I wanted this Florida move to work for both of us, so I finally agreed that I would help her get started. I filled out the IRS application for a 501(c)(3) public charity, and soon afterward Mary Ellen received a letter of approval. Golden Rescue in Naples, Inc.—or GRINinc, as the rescue was informally known—came into existence. I was assigned the job of chief assistant to the president/founder, who was Mary Ellen. She then appointed me treasurer. We passed out fliers with the GRINinc logo, and word quickly got out that there was a golden retriever rescue starting in Naples. Before long, she had a full list of volunteers. Some offered to serve as fosters and others as transporters. A few had dog-rescue experience, so they were assigned to handle the intakes, screen prospective adopters, and do home visits.

We ordered a supply of collars and dog tags, we had application forms printed, and we got a huge bag of tennis balls from the tennis pro at our club. They had been used and discarded, but the retrievers would not know the difference. Each dog would be given a tennis ball on arrival. It was all coming together.

Here's something else I've learned about dog lovers everywhere: they can be very generous. Volunteers and members stepped up and supported GRINinc through donations and annual membership dues, and soon the rescue was financially sound. Paying the bills was never a problem. Later on, if GRINinc got short on funds, a few words about its needs in the biannual newsletter usually did the job. This allowed Mary Ellen and the board to concentrate on saving dogs. In time, GRINinc would serve a large geographic area extending from Sarasota down to Naples on the west coast of Florida and over to Miami on the east coast. At its peak, GRINinc would boast between fifty and sixty volunteers and more than two hundred members. By its ten-year anniversary, GRINinc had rescued more than five hundred dogs. But before all that was the beginning.

Mary Ellen introducing each owner & dog

Parade of Rescue Dogs

Reunion

Bridget, Skidder and Sandy

Carrie

Allie

Pilot and friend

Amelia

Jetta

Lucky

Rose

Logo

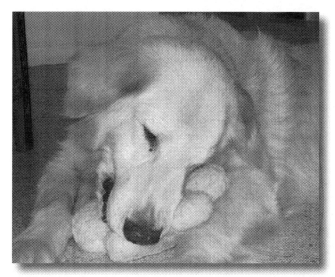

Sarge

Annie

Buster

Topper

Charlie swimming

Mama Sam

Teddy on arrival

Teddy one year later

Mary Ellen and Casey

The Early Days

GRININC WAS JUST GETTING STARTED, AND AL-
ready it was getting busy. Before long, we would be in high gear.
But first, we had a lot to learn about Florida. It was significantly
different from Ohio in many ways.

Early on, a realtor had called GRINinc to say that a family
had moved out of one of her rental houses and taken all their
belongings except for their dog. As is typical in Florida, this
house had a screened lanai. When the realtor came to inspect
the house and ready it for a new tenant, she found that a golden
retriever had been left on the lanai, abandoned. The family had
not even bothered to call or leave a note. The dog had no collar
and no tags. All they left was her water bowl, and that was empty.

This would not be the only dog we rescued after a family
moved and left it behind. I've never been able to grasp the mind-
set of someone who could do that—leave a dog to fend for itself
in the hot, humid Florida weather. In another case, it was a week
before a neighbor noticed that the house next door was empty
and there was a dog lying on the lanai. By the time we got there,
the dog was in bad shape, having gone without food and water
for days. But remarkably, the dog lived.

Initially, GRINinc had a lot of intakes that were very similar.
The Naples area was a favorite spot for retired couples, and

many of them had dogs for companionship. The couples would get up in years, and suddenly one spouse would take sick and go to a nursing home, the other would move to an assisted-living facility, and their dog would need a new home. These dogs were trained and well cared for, and most were medically sound. Finding a new home was not at all difficult, because other newly retired couples relocating to the Naples area were looking for a companion and did not want to train a puppy. Puppies were too active and too strong; they could injure older people by pulling them over. So these couples were looking for a well-mannered young or adult dog and thus turned to the rescue organizations. These were the easy and straightforward adoptions.

The classifieds and Craigslist were other good places to find displaced golden retrievers. I once saw an ad on Craigslist that said, "I will trade my golden retriever puppy for a Sea-Doo." Some owners who were being forced to relinquish their pets or did not want them anymore would decide that selling their dogs, rather than finding them good homes, was an appealing idea. A volunteer was assigned to monitor the newspaper and the Internet to look for those ads. Then the volunteer would call the owner and offer the rescue's services. Often the owner would blow the volunteer off, but other times the owner would agree to give the dog to the rescue. Sometimes it took a little haggling and negotiation—fifty or seventy-five dollars usually did the trick.

If dog fighting was going on in Ohio, we were never aware of it. But it did go on in Florida. Most often, pit bulls were used in the ring, but other breeds were used to bait and train those dogs for fighting. It was not unusual for stolen dogs or pets given away for free in the classifieds to end up being used in this way. A docile pet that had never even growled at another dog would disappear from its owner's yard and end up being thrown into a dog-fighting ring and torn apart. Other owners, believing they had found their pets loving new homes, would be saddened to hear that the dogs had ended up in a pit bull ring.

Some of these dogs would fight back to save themselves and survive; after a time, they would be turned loose with their injuries and allowed to wander off. Some would be found and turned in to animal shelters and make their way to rescue. But with no tags and no chips, it was impossible to find the owners. Who knew where these dogs had come from or who their real owners were?

Often, stolen dogs were transported across several states before being sold to people in the dog-fighting business. The practice was ugly and repulsive, and when a dog-fighting ring was uncovered and exposed, the public was understandably outraged; yet it continued. Rehabilitating these bait dogs was a long and arduous process. It was not only the physical wounds but also the emotional wounds that needed tending. Both left scars that healed slowly. It took a lot of time and special nursing before these dogs recovered. They were wary of strangers and clung to their new owners. Who could blame them if they had difficulty trusting someone they did not know?

Seldom did the principals of a dog-fighting ring ever go to jail. It was a close-knit community and difficult for outsiders to penetrate. When one ring got closed down, another would quickly form and take its place.

Rose

ONE DAY MARY ELLEN NOTICED AN AD IN THE classified section of the newspaper: "Scruffy one-eyed but lovable 4 yr. old Golden Retriever female … free." She called the phone number listed in the ad. The owner was a breeder located on the edge of the Everglades, and the dog's name was Rose. She was an outside dog and his breeding bitch, and he no longer wanted her. He gave Mary Ellen directions to his farm and ended the conversation by saying, "I'm giving her away to the first person who gets here, but if you don't come by noon, I will need to destroy her."

So off Mary Ellen went to rescue her first dog in Florida, having no idea what deplorable conditions she would find. We were new to Naples, and the Everglades are not easy to navigate. Referring to the directions she had written down from the breeder, she found herself on curving dirt roads that took her deeper and deeper into the Everglades and eventually led her to the farm where Rose and seventeen other dogs roamed freely.

Mary Ellen observed the overgrown jungle where the dogs lived. They were mostly retrievers—goldens and Labradors. The only shelter was an occasional palm tree or a bush. All they had to quench their thirst was some green water in a large, dirty bucket, and their food rested in a dirty trough. The dogs were at all stages of development: puppies, adults, and pregnant mothers. They all had thin coats and open sores; flies followed them everywhere.

The dogs were friendly and greeted Mary Ellen. Out came the owner, who whistled for Rose. She came, very slowly. The poor dog was drained of life and had none of the exuberance you typically find in a golden retriever. She was very scruffy and covered with open sores. Her right eye was sunk deep into her skull, oozing from an infection. She had been bred continually since she was seven months old, and the deplorable life she led had taken its toll.

Mary Ellen would gladly have taken all the dogs, but the owner would only part with Rose, and so she lifted the dog into her car and drove to Dr. Stacey's office.

Dr. Stacey was a young veterinarian who was just getting started, like GRINinc. Mary Ellen had visited most of the veterinarians in the Naples area, and Dr. Stacey had impressed her the most. Mary Ellen was pleased that the doctor was willing to work with the rescue and had offered her services. Mary Ellen was eager to develop a working relationship between Dr. Stacey and the rescue, and Rose would be their first collaboration.

Dr. Stacey examined Rose and then looked at Mary Ellen and said, "I hope all your rescues aren't this bad."

"You should see what I left behind," Mary Ellen replied.

"Rose will require a good deal of nursing care after she is discharged," Dr. Stacey added.

It took three baths to remove the fleas and stench from Rose. After three weeks of antibiotics, during which time she became stronger and healthier, she underwent a four-hour surgery to spay her and remove her damaged eye. During the surgery, it became obvious to Dr. Stacey that the injury was the result of blunt trauma. Someone had hit this dog.

In time, Rose blossomed into a sweet, lovable, and loyal

golden. Brandishing her one eye and an infectious smile, she became the mascot and poster child of Golden Rescue in Naples, Inc., with her distinctive face. She survived because she was strong and independent—qualities she shared with her rescuer.

Initially, Rose was adopted out to a neighbor and friend of ours, and so she lived nearby. Whenever she saw Mary Ellen in the neighborhood, she would give out a high bark, climb into Mary Ellen's arms, give her kisses, and cuddle. Sometime later, the adopter, Ken, developed cancer and died. He made Mary Ellen promise to take Rose when he passed, and so Rose came back to our home to live out her days with her one good eye following Mary Ellen everywhere. Rose was constantly at her side.

Dr. Stacey went on to become one of the most successful veterinarians in Southwest Florida. She expanded her office into a full-service clinic and added three more veterinarians to handle the volume of patients. Through the years, she proved to be an invaluable asset to GRINinc. Mary Ellen and Dr. Stacey shared many patients over those years, but neither of them ever forgot Rose and the challenge she presented.

Years later, a bank foreclosure forced the puppy farm to close. When the public became aware of what had transpired, there was an outcry over Rose's breeder. Mary Ellen and others had filed complaints against him, but nothing was ever done to close this breeder down. The public demanded to know where Domestic Animal Services had been, as it was the county agency empowered to enforce laws protecting animals. How could its animal control officers have allowed this travesty to go on for years?

At public hearings, Mary Ellen and others told of witnessing firsthand the deplorable, disgusting conditions at this breeding farm. If it did not fit the description of abuse and neglect, then nothing did. Why had it taken a foreclosure to put an end to the operation?

People looking to buy a puppy would answer this breeder's ad in the classified section of the newspaper and ultimately find their way to the farm. Most were repulsed by what they found and quickly got into their cars and left. A few were overcome with compassion and paid the breeder his asking price of a few hundred dollars. They couldn't save all the puppies, but at least they could save one. They would take the puppy to their veterinarian, and like Rose, it would be given vaccines and antibiotics and several baths to remove the stench before it was ready to be taken home.

While many of these puppies went on to live long and happy lives, no one who visited that farm could forget the ones that were left behind—the unfortunate dogs that never made it out of this breeder's hellhole, the ones that suffered and died from disease and neglect. Complaints were filed, yet nothing was done to close the breeder down or force him to clean up his act.

At the public hearings, the records of Domestic Animal Services revealed that its control officers would respond to the complaints by paying a visit to the farm and leaving a citation. There was little evidence of follow-up to see if the breeder had complied with the citation. And so it continued on for years until the breeder lost his farm to a bank foreclosure, the dogs were turned in to Labrador and golden retriever rescues, and the public became aware of the ugly facts of what had transpired. The director of Domestic Animal Services attempted to defend her stewardship, but it was pure bureaucratic double-talk. There was no reasonable explanation or excuse for what had happened under her watch except for negligence.

The room in which the public hearings were held was packed with an overflow crowd. When it was Mary Ellen's turn to talk, she went to the podium and not only detailed Rose's story but also criticized the agency for the manner in which it had handled this breeder and for the years it had allowed him to continue. She quickly overran her allotted time to speak, and the committee chairman asked her to sit down.

The audience started shouting, "Let her speak! Let her finish!" First one and then another speaker said, "I relinquish my time to her."

Calmly, Mary Ellen continued, saying, "I am not sitting down until you have heard everything."

With that, one of the Domestic Animal Services staff members got up and left the room. Before long, two large county sheriff's deputies showed up. I fully expected them to haul Mary Ellen away in handcuffs, but she had just finished when they arrived.

There was an irony there that everyone in attendance recognized: Domestic Animal Services had allowed a law-breaking breeder to ignore citations and defy them for years, but they did not hesitate to call the sheriff on a 112-pound dog rescuer who refused to stop speaking and sit down. Perhaps they did not want to hear what she had to say.

Through its Domestic Animal Services agency, the county is responsible for enforcing the laws protecting pets as well as the public. There are not many regulations for domestic animals, but they must be licensed each year and vaccinated against rabies every three years. They must not be allowed to run free, they must be provided some sort of shelter, and most important, they must not be abused. Animal cruelty laws are not specific, however, and animal control officers sometimes see cruelty and abuse differently than the average person does. If animal control officers everywhere were chosen for their love of and compassion for animals, things would be different. Too often the position of director or control officer becomes available and someone is given the job because he or she is next on the list. Regrettably, new employees are rarely matched to those positions the way new owners are matched to rescue dogs.

What happened next was typical of government everywhere. Government employees are never fired for incompetence; they are just reassigned. So instead of firing this director, the County Board of Commissioners, which oversaw the director and the agency, quietly removed her and put her in charge of another county agency.

This chapter is in no way meant to condemn all animal control directors or officers or the agencies they work for. Most such agencies are managed professionally, and many, if not most, officers and their directors are dedicated and do an excellent job carrying out their duties. We applaud them.

Sarge

DURING THE TIME WHEN WE WERE NURSING Rose back to health, we got a call from a man who said a friend of his—a Vietnam veteran who owned a golden retriever—had had a serious heart attack, was in the hospital, and was not coming home. The caller owned a pizza shop and could not care for the dog himself, and he could not find anyone else to take the dog. The dog was living in the veteran's yard. Sometimes the pizza shop owner got there to feed it, sometimes not. No one was caring for the dog. Could we help?

It was the Fourth of July weekend, and severe storms were forecast, so we drove to the pizza shop for dinner and talked to the owner.

"As far as I know, the dog is in good health and very friendly," he said. "My friend had no family and few friends and lived alone. Actually, the dog was all he had and was his constant companion." Then he told us where we could find the dog and signed the release forms.

It was late and dark when we found the small house. There was no light anywhere as we made our way to the rear yard. Neighbors were firing off firecrackers, and we could hear the distant thunder of an impending storm. We entered the darkened yard not knowing what we'd find—but what we did not find was the dog. We called and called, but he did not appear.

I looked at my wife and said, "What do you want to do? Is there some way we can contact the friend at the pizza shop? Do you think he just ran off?"

"I'm not sure what we should do," she answered. "I suppose we could check with the neighbors and see if someone took him into their house, but no one seems to be around."

We decided to give up, but just as we turned to leave, a Roman candle burst overhead and we saw the dog huddled in the far corner of the yard, trembling in fear. We knelt and petted him. It was obvious that he was a wreck from the fireworks and terrified of the noise. As we got him up to take him with us, we looked him over. There was one big problem: this dog was mostly Labrador retriever and a mix of other breeds. People who contacted our golden retriever rescue looking to adopt wanted golden retrievers, not Labradors.

Then we thought of the impending thunderstorms and his thunder-phobia. We couldn't just leave him, and so we carried him to the car.

We found adopters on the east coast who didn't care that he was a mixed breed or what he looked like. We renamed him Sarge and drove him across Alligator Alley to his new home. Later we wrote a short story about his new life and how well he was doing. We put this into an envelope along with some pictures and dropped it off at the pizza shop, where the owner took it and gave it to his friend the Vietnam vet, who was recovering in a nursing home.

Annie

ANNIE WAS A SMALL SENIOR FEMALE WHO weighed about fifty pounds and had come into GRINinc from a shelter. Not much was known about her—the rescue workers named her Annie—but the first thing everyone noticed was that she was missing her front teeth, both upper and lower. That seemed strange.

She sported a light-red coat and was full of energy, and it became obvious that she had never received any obedience training. In truth, she was a dynamo. The rescue could not find anyone to willing take her as a foster, because no one could handle her.

After Rose's adopter—our neighbor, Ken—died, his partner, Jim, decided to move into a new house. The house he had shared with Ken had not sold and was empty. A cute detached cabana off the pool lanai featured a small living room, bedroom, kitchen, and bath. It was perfect for a mother-in-law or guests. Jim was an animal lover and owned several small pets, and when he became aware that Mary Ellen was having a problem placing Annie in a foster home, he called her and said, "Just put her in the cabana until you find a home for her."

"Are you sure you want to do that?" Mary Ellen asked.

"Why not?" he replied. "What can happen? Keep her there and use it as long as you need it."

With Jim's encouragement, Mary Ellen put Annie in the cabana. A volunteer was given the key and the job of visiting her several times a day, feeding her, giving her fresh water, and exercising her. It sure sounded like the perfect solution at the time.

Later in the day, the phone rang. It was Mary, the volunteer, on her first visit to the cabana to see Annie.

"Mary Ellen, you better come right over."

"Is there a problem?"

"Just get over here."

Wondering what it was all about, Mary Ellen went over to the house and walked into the cabana. She looked around and her heart sank. Scanning all the rooms, she saw nothing but carnage and destruction. The cute cabana was destroyed. Kitchen cabinet doors were hanging open at odd angles, and the dishwasher door was lying on the floor. Everything in the living room and bedroom had been attacked and thrown about. Annie had been so busy that she was exhausted; now she was resting on the floor, panting.

Mary, the volunteer, was in shock, and all Mary Ellen could do was sit down and put her face in her hands. Now they knew why Annie did not have any teeth.

The first thing Mary Ellen had to do was call Jim. She wondered if the damage was covered by the rescue's insurance. If not, where would she find the funds to pay for the damage? It was going to take a lot of money to repair and replace just about everything in the cabana.

It wasn't long before Jim arrived. He gave the cabana a quick walk-through, but his reaction was not at all what the women expected.

"Forget it," he told them. "She can't do any more damage, so just keep her here. After you place her, I will get everything repaired and replaced and fixed up, and it will look better that it did before. Who knows, maybe my homeowners' insurance will cover it."

The rescue's veterinarian prescribed some medication to keep Annie calm, and so it was that Annie stayed in the cabana until they found her a new owner—and that was not easy.

There was not much left to destroy in the cabana, so there were no more surprises. The medication did its job, and Mary and Mary Ellen shared the duty of visiting and caring for Annie until the challenge of finding her a new home could be met. Annie was finally adopted out to a no-nonsense guy who promptly took her to obedience training and then repeated the classes two more times until she finally got the message. The new owner was a contractor, and he planned on taking Annie with him on his rounds as he inspected the progress on his jobs. She would spend the day with him as a companion and ride in his truck.

The board of the rescue thought his being a contractor was a bonus, as presumably he could repair any future damage Annie inflicted should she have a relapse. The new owner, however, worked wonders, transforming Annie the dynamo into Annie the quiet, truck-riding companion. Everyone marveled at the new Annie, because when she smiled and revealed her missing teeth, they remembered the wild lady who destroyed the cabana.

Buster

WHEN GRININC STARTED IN NAPLES, DOGS could be tethered to anything in the yard and left out all day in the heat. They also could be put into an open truck, free from any restraint. They were often injured if the truck was in an accident, or sometimes the truck could be stopped at a traffic light and something would spook the dog, causing it to jump out, dart into traffic, and get hit by a passing car. You could point out the dangers of leaving a dog chained outside all day or explain why dogs needed to be crated when riding in an open vehicle, but most owners would just wave you off with one finger.

Dog lovers share many qualities, including advocacy, activism, and persistence, and if laws are needed to protect dogs, they can very persistent. They can also be annoying and labeled pests, but that doesn't bother them. So it was not remarkable that dog lovers and various rescue organizations of Southwest Florida ultimately came together to get tethering and open vehicle laws passed. Both laws were badly needed, but it took years before county commissioners finally passed legislation that a dog could not be tethered and left outside, and if it was transported in an open truck or vehicle, it needed to be in a crate. Some say the commissioners were tired of hearing about it—that they were weary of the calls and visits from constituents pressing the issue—but the laws were passed, and as a result, the lives of many dogs improved and those of other dogs were saved.

Before that legislation, it was common in Florida to see a dog left chained to a tree. One man who lived on the edge of the Everglades kept his golden retriever chained to a piling on his boat ramp. No one ever saw the dog off the chain or witnessed any interaction between the dog and his owner; they were never observed walking or playing together. Once a day, the owner put out some food and replenished the water. This dog led a miserable life under the boat ramp, devoid of contact and interaction with anyone. Neighbors would see him out there every day and feel horrible for him. No question that he was friendly—he would wag his tail as they passed—but because of the cranky owner, few people approached him.

They knew his name: Buster. Cleaned up and brushed, he would have resembled the dog in the Bush's Baked Beans commercials. Everyone wished that someone could relieve this kind and gentle dog of his awful existence and that he would end up with someone who would love and appreciate him. His plight was reported to animal services, but nothing came of it.

Rescues and other organizations would show up from time to time and talk to the owner, telling him, "If you don't want the dog, give him up and we will find him a good home."

His answer was always the same: "Mind your own business."

Owners like this are stubborn; the more they are pushed, the more obstinate they become. They dig in their heels. No one is going to tell them what to do with their dog. They almost relish being defiant. It is a control issue: they seem to enjoy the role of being mean and nasty and daring anyone to stop them. It would take a good psychiatrist to explain why they seem to derive satisfaction from the suffering they inflict, or why they are so uncaring and devoid of compassion.

Each time situations like Buster's were discussed, someone

would say, "What is wrong with these people?" and no one seemed to have an answer. Then someone would point out that it was not uncommon for people to treat other human beings just as badly or worse.

Human nature apparently has a dark side where meanness and cruelty replace compassion and love. Not all who abuse animals progress to more serious episodes involving their fellow human beings, but too many start out that way. That behavior is something society cannot and should not tolerate. Exposing animal abuse and those who are guilty of it is the first step in stopping it. As I said, it would be nice if all dog owners were required to be, at the very least, dog likers.

Two young locals—"good old boys," as people called them— drove past Buster as they went to and from work every day. Twice a day, Buster would watch them as their truck approached, and as they passed by, he would bark and wag his tail frantically. Other times when their truck passed, they would see Buster lying under the ramp. After a while, Buster and his sad, dismal life started to bother these two locals. Who knows, maybe they were dog lovers and did not realize it, but regardless, there came a time when they just couldn't take seeing Buster live like that anymore. Passing him every day and watching him wag his tail was beginning to wear on them, and they decided to do something about it.

One day they showed up at one of the shelters with a golden retriever on a leash. They were lean and tall and dressed in jeans, soiled T-shirts, boots, and work hats sporting the names of power tools above the bills. They were overdue for a haircut and a shave. One was chewing tobacco, or maybe it was snuff; the clerk could not decide. She could see their beat-up Ford 150 pickup, gun rack attached, parked outside.

"His name is Buster, and we want you to find him a good home," one of the men offered.

The clerk started filling out the intake forms. "How long have you had him?"

"We just got him. His owner just gave him to us."

"Where is the dog from?"

"Out at the edge of Big Cypress Reservation."

The clerk looked up at them. "Is this Buster the dog kept out under the boat ramp?"

They both chimed in, "Yes ma'am, that's him."

The clerk smiled. "Everyone has tried to get Buster," she said. "How did you ever get the owner to give him to you?"

"Well, first we got the owner's attention, and then we talked to him real nice."

With that, the men signed the forms and left.

No one knows what transpired when the locals pulled up at the boat ramp in their old pickup. It is possible that the gun rack was full when they spoke with Buster's owner, but we likely will never know. What we do know is that the shelter where the locals left him called GRINinc to tell us they had a dog for us.

When we found out the dog was Buster, everyone was shocked. We were aware of other situations like Buster's, where a dog was abused and neglected but we were unable to help. I believe Mary Ellen and the other volunteers had resolved that nothing could be done for Buster and decided to concentrate their efforts on those instances where they felt they could effect a change. They'd had no choice but to accept that Buster's situation would never change; they'd discussed him, and in the end the owner's intransigence seemed to be a roadblock that they could not overcome. Having tried to rescue Buster many times, they never thought that change would ever happen for him—but here he was, and his life would change dramatically. Finally getting a dog like Buster was an exception and something to celebrate.

On the list of adopters was a fishing captain who was looking for a companion that he could take with him on the boat when he guided his fishing clients. Buster was a great match. Every day, wearing his life vest, Buster would hop on the boat and greet the fishermen as they boarded, and then he would ride along in the first mate's seat and bark as each fish was brought to the boat. When the fishing trip was finished, Buster would sit and watch the captain as he cleaned the fish, making sure to bark at the pelicans and keep them away. Pelicans routinely hung around the fish-cleaning station at the docks, eating what was discarded and stealing a fish or two when the opportunity presented itself. One thing about Buster: he knew his way around boat ramps, and there would be no fish-stealing as long as he was around. Then, when the day was done, side by side they would go, the captain and Buster with his tail wagging.

Occasionally, Buster and the captain would be out on the water and would pass Captain Bruce, one of the best fishing guides in Southwest Florida. Bruce had his own tale of rescuing a dog, but it was much different from Buster's story.

One day Bruce's wife brought home a Labrador puppy. He was barely eight weeks old, puppy-cute, and full of energy. They had not even decided on a name for him when, the following day, Bruce boarded the fishing boat that he kept tied to a dock at the rear of his property. He was about to pull away from the dock when the puppy came bounding down from the house, jumping and barking and carrying on, wanting to go with him. That day Bruce had only one client; they'd planned to go fly-fishing in the backwaters. He normally would not take a dog with him when he was working as a guide, but this time he relented. He reached over and picked the pup up off the dock and put him on the boat, and off they went.

Bruce made a quick stop to pick up his client, and then he proceeded to navigate the narrow channels that would lead them to the fishing spots he had selected. Meanwhile, the puppy was scooting about the boat, enjoying every minute. The channels wound their way through thousands of islands that were overgrown with mangrove trees. Hanging his paws over one side of the boat, the puppy would search the mangroves on the nearby shoreline for a while and then run over to the other side to check the other shoreline.

That day, Bruce and his client were fishing for mackerel. The fish were in a school, and from time to time the school would move en masse another fifty or so yards away from the boat. When that happened, Bruce would engage the idling outboard motor and quickly propel the boat to where the mackerel had moved. They had just moved to a new spot and were casting off the bow when Bruce turned to check on the puppy and found that the back of the boat was empty. The puppy was gone.

The men quickly put down their rods and searched the water, but the puppy was nowhere to be found. Bruce turned the boat around and slowly began retracing his route, using the wake as a guide. As he moved along he continued searching, but there was no sign of the puppy. Apparently, when Bruce gunned the motor to move to a new spot, the puppy had been thrown off the boat. But where and when did it happen? By now the boat had moved a good distance and its wake was hardly recognizable. Bruce got a sick feeling in his stomach. He thought about going home and telling his wife that the puppy was gone.

Good guides are blessed with unusually good eyesight, and Bruce was no exception. A client would cast high into the mangroves lining the shore and tell Bruce, "My hook is somewhere up in the mangroves, but I don't know where," and Bruce would scan the trees and say, "I see it."

"Where?" the client would ask.

"Second mangrove tree from the left, fourth branch up from the bottom on the right," Bruce would answer, and sure enough, there it was.

Bruce continued to let the boat creep along the narrow channel, and suddenly he spotted a slight movement off to the side. It resembled a large bug or maybe a leaf, but it was moving ever so slightly. It was something only someone with Bruce's eyesight could see. Alerted, he focused on the spot and maneuvered the boat over to the side of the channel. As he got closer, he saw that the bug was the puppy's nose. The puppy was not horizontal but vertical in the water, with only his nose sticking out. He was barely moving his paws, trying to tread water and keep from going under. Who knew how long he had been there.

Bruce reached down, grabbed the puppy by the scruff of the neck, and lifted him out of the water. The puppy was so exhausted he could not stand or whimper. He was gasping for air and could not have lasted much longer. Bruce put the puppy in his lap and headed for home. They'd had enough excitement for one day. The sight of the puppy's nose, and the thought of how close they'd come to losing him, haunted Bruce for some time.

Reunion

ONCE A YEAR, GRININC HELD A REUNION WHERE many of the rescue dogs and their adopters would gather. It was always in January or February, when the weather was cool and the dogs as well as their owners could be comfortable in an outdoor setting. Even though some adopters had moved from the Naples area, they would load up their campers and drive for hours, or even days, just to attend the event. They forged friendships at these reunions and looked forward to returning so they could catch up and exchange stories about their rescue dogs with someone who understood completely their devotion to their goldens.

Laurie, one of the volunteers, lived away from the city on a piece of property large enough to accommodate everything GRINinc needed for its reunion, including a spacious area off to the side for parking and Porta-Potties. A big tent would be set up, along with park benches and tables. The cool weather kept the dogs active and frisky, so the owners could let them chase tennis balls and play with each other without concern.

After a couple of hours of socializing, the grills were fired up and the usual lunch of hot dogs, burgers, and potato salad was served. After lunch, the crowd would gather around for the Parade of Rescue Dogs. Leading the parade would be Rose, the rescue's unofficial mascot. Rose was a constant reminder that all the effort and hard work put forth in saving dogs was worth it. The parade was the highlight of the reunion and what everyone anticipated most.

Owners of rescue dogs share a special bond with each other as well as with their dogs. There is an unspoken understanding between them; they will tell you that only someone who has experienced the rescue process can fully appreciate what another owner has gone through. They describe it as a life-changing experience. After a reunion is over, owners will keep in touch via e-mail, sharing photos and updating each other on their dogs' lives, informing them of illnesses and other changes. Quite often when a rescue dog finally passes over the Rainbow Bridge, its passing will be mourned by many other owners who knew of the dog. And after the passing of their rescue pet, many owners start all over again with a new rescue pet, so the process renews itself.

As I have said, owners who take in rescue dogs are a special breed of dog lovers. They share an innate passion and motivation that dog likers cannot completely understand but other dog lovers recognize and identify with.

Rescuer Recognition

YOU HAVE TO IMAGINE WHAT IT IS LIKE FOR A dog to be abandoned. As someone's pet, you are given shelter; you are fed and cared for when you're sick. This is the only life you know. Then suddenly one day, you are taken for a ride, the car door opens, and after you step out, the car drives off. You find yourself alone and confused. What has happened to you? Where has everyone who used to care for you gone?

You are now on your own for food and shelter. You wander around, trying to find your way home, not knowing where you are. You become thirsty and look for water. You become hungry and cannot find food. You are cold and look for shelter. You walk into the street and are almost hit by a passing car because you do not know any better. Many people are afraid of dogs, and so when you approach them, they chase you off. Others do not recognize your plight, nor do they care, so they ignore you.

You become homeless, searching for food every day and taking shelter wherever you can find it. You smell discarded food around a dumpster in an alley, but when you get there, a small pack of dogs are already there, and they are not about to share the few morsels with you. They snarl and you move on. Adults chase you away, and kids who do not know better are mean to you. If you are sick or injured, no one cares for you; you suffer silently. It is a miserable existence with no future.

If you are one of the fortunate ones, however, someone walks up to you and pets you one day. She rubs her hand on the back of your head; it's a gesture you recognize. She gives you water and food and brings you to a shelter or calls a rescue organization to pick you up. From that day on, your life has changed again. No more wandering aimlessly, looking for water and food. No more dirty, thin coat with ribs sticking out from your underweight body. You have found someone to care for you and give you a new life. You have been rescued.

When a dog is rescued, especially under adverse conditions, the person who rescues the dog is forever burned into its memory. The dog remembers his voice, the way he walks, and how he smells. The dog remembers that it was this man who first stroked its head and gave it comfort, and maybe provided its first meal in a long time, along with shelter and security. Rescue dogs remember who took them from miserable conditions to a safe, happy, loving home. They do not forget the rescuer who gave them a secure environment with a new family that will love and care for them.

Many of these first rescuers maintain contact with the adopters. They are also forever bonded with the dogs they have saved. Like the dogs, they also remember the circumstances of their first meeting. Years later, a rescuer can enter a room, and if a dog she has rescued is off in the corner, it will hear her voice and observe her walk and immediately its demeanor will change. It could have been standing or lying quietly, but now its head and ears will go up, it will stand tall on its pads, and its whole body will stiffen. It will lean forward for a better look, and then, recognizing the sound of the approaching rescuer's voice, the dog will rush forward, barking, jumping, and carrying on.

There is only one way to quiet a dog in these circumstances:

the rescuer has to bend down to hug and acknowledge it. With that, the dog will start jumping and dancing and planting endless kisses on the rescuer's face. This is the greeting a rescuer will receive, regardless how long it has been since she and the dog last saw each other.

"Rescuer recognition" is well known and has been experienced by every rescuer in the dog-saving business. Folklore has it that there is a special section in heaven, just over the Rainbow Bridge, where dog rescuers and the dogs they rescued will meet. And if you tell dog rescuers that dogs don't go to heaven, they will gladly tell you that in that case, they don't want to go there either. They want to go wherever the dogs are.

Topper

ONE STORY HIGHLIGHTS RESCUER RECOGNITION
in a very special way. A state wildlife agent making his rounds
in a wooded area found a golden retriever with one leg snared in
an animal trap. In his years as a ranger, he had found all sorts
of wildlife in the traps, but never a dog. He bent down and found
that the dog was so weak and emaciated it could hardly move.
Who knew how long the dog had been there or how long it had
been without food and water.

The agent released the dog's leg from the snare and gave
it all the water in the bottle he carried on his belt. Then he
wrapped it in a blanket, put it in his van, and dropped it off at a
veterinarian's office to see if the leg and the dog could be saved.
At the time, the ranger did not hold out much hope, and so he
was surprised when the veterinarian was able to mend the leg
and nurse the dog back to health.

In time, the dog—a young male—regained its agility, although it sported a permanent limp. But this dog would not let
his gimpy leg hold him back.

The dog was not chipped, and the veterinarian's office
checked everywhere to see if a golden retriever had been reported missing. They checked all the usual places, but it was a

familiar story: this dog had simply been dropped off and left to fend for himself.

The ranger would call the vet's office regularly to check on the dog's progress, and so the office staff asked him if he wanted to name the dog.

"He's the tops," said the ranger. "Just call him Topper—and find him a good home."

The ranger never forgot Topper, and he followed the dog's progress by maintaining contact after Topper was turned over to our rescue. From time to time he would call to inquire about the dog, and so the rescue invited the ranger to an upcoming reunion, since Topper would be there. At the end of the Parade of Rescue Dogs, the ranger joined Mary Ellen and called out to Topper, who was at his owner's feet, sleeping under a bench. Hearing the ranger's voice, Topper jumped up and searched the crowd until he found his rescuer. Topper's owner dropped the leash, and gimpy Topper rushed over to greet the agent. The agent hadn't changed, but Topper was different. His leg was healed, he was groomed, and he had put on some weight.

He also wore a vest now. He had been trained as a therapy dog, and his owner would take him to visit elderly people who were lonely and residing in assisted-living facilities. These people had been forced to give up their companions because dogs were not allowed there. Topper would approach a seated resident and gently place his gimpy left leg, which pointed out at an odd angle, on his or her lap. It was Topper's way of saying hello. He would canvass the activities room, moving from one resident to another and pausing to greet each one and present his paw, and they in turn would say, "Well hello, Topper! And how are you today?" A few pats on the head, and he would move on to the next resident.

This ranger and this dog were forever linked, and it would stay that way. From time to time, the rescue's phone would ring and the caller would say, "How is Topper getting along?"

Charlie

SURPRISINGLY, MANY GOLDEN RETRIEVERS DO
not like water and do not swim, although those that are introduced to water and learn to swim as puppies generally enjoy
it. If you attempt to train an adult golden to swim, you will find
that it's as fearful and reluctant to enter the water as most other
dogs. But every once in a while, you'll come across a dog that
was just *born to swim*. You can't keep it out of the water. It sees
a pool, pond, lake, or canal, and if not restrained, in it will go. It
will swim to its heart's content, and you can't get it to stop.

Charlie was the only retriever we met that fit this description.
Charlie was *born to swim*.

One day, a couple noticed a dog swimming in the lake behind
their property. They did not think much of it until they observed
him there the next day. He just kept swimming about, up and
down the lake. *Who is this dog, and where did he come from?* they
wondered.

In Florida there is an adage: "Where there is water, there
are alligators." The couple feared that this dog would become
a meal, so they talked to their neighbors, attempting to find out
who owned him. One neighbor said she'd seen a car pull up, let
the dog out, and drive off. That was a couple of days earlier, and

the dog had been hanging around and swimming in the lake ever since.

Returning to their yard, the couple found the dog lying on the grass, exhausted. They put him in the car and dropped him off at a veterinarian's office, where he slept for two days. He was a gentle, middle-aged male and appeared to be in good health. It was hard to imagine why his owners had just abandoned him.

The veterinarian's office turned him over to Mary Ellen, who named him Charlie and brought him home to foster, hoping he would fit in with our two males, Alfie and Comet (who was still with us at the time). We introduced Charlie to his new family and showed him his new house, and then we walked him out to our lanai. Charlie took one look at our pool and promptly jumped in and began swimming laps. Back and forth he went with a big smile on his face, throwing his head back and barking a high-pitched, happy bark. Charlie did not glide through the water; rather, he slapped the water with his front paws, splashing his way around the pool, with Alfie and Comet running along the edge, barking and urging him on. (Neither Alfie nor Comet swam; the only way to get them into the water was to carry them.)

From time to time, Charlie would turn and swim over to where Alfie and Comet were leaning over the side of the pool. Then he would slap the water repeatedly with his paw, splashing both of them in the face, and they would jump back and bark louder. On and on this circus continued. All three were having a grand old time.

There was one problem: Charlie would not come out. We waited for him to tire, but he showed no signs of it. Finally I donned my bathing suit and went into the pool. It took some time to corner him, but eventually I was able to grab him by the collar and drag him up the steps. He was so exhausted from the exercise that his legs were wobbling and he could hardly stand.

Each day when I returned home from the golf course, I would

find Charlie sitting on the pool deck. Mary Ellen had decided that if Charlie was going to swim, he needed to wear a life vest. As soon as he saw me, he would go over and bark at his swimming vest lying nearby, and he would continue to bark until I put the vest on him.

Charlie could get depressed if a day passed and he did not swim, but once he had his vest on, he knew it was swimming time. So as soon as he was suited up, he would throw his outstretched body into the pool and begin swimming his laps—up and down, back and forth. Soon the pool deck would come alive with dogs barking and water flying everywhere.

In time it became obvious that Charlie wasn't going anywhere and we had a new addition to our family. And Mary Ellen had another name to add to her list. Just call her a "failed foster mom."

We were concerned that Charlie's barking when he swam, and all the commotion it caused with the other dogs barking and urging him on, would bother our neighbors. We spoke with them and always got the same response: "Don't worry—we didn't hear anything." However, they did appreciate the fact that we'd expressed concern that they might have been bothered.

Keeping the Peace

WE HAD LIVED IN SEVERAL HOMES IN OHIO AND, later, in Florida, and we were fortunate that our dogs never caused any issues with our neighbors. Looking back, I can't recall a single instance of friction or dissention with our neighbors that was caused by our having dogs as pets. For the most part, we found that our neighbors enjoyed having the dogs nearby. They accepted our dogs as they would have accepted a family with children. The key was that the dogs did not bother them in any way.

Much of the credit rests with Mary Ellen, who is the epitome of a responsible dog owner. She did not allow our dogs to bark or disturb those who lived around us, and she made sure to pick up after them on walks. There was no jumping when they met or passed someone on their strolls. If someone wanted to stop and meet or pet the dogs, that was fine; otherwise, Mary Ellen made sure the dogs did not hinder or bother anyone they encountered on their daily walks. She kept them well behaved and well trained—a practice she tried to instill in fosters and prospective adopters as well, as it makes for a peaceful life with neighbors. In her discussions with adopters, Mary Ellen could be a little preachy on the subject of being a responsible dog owner, but they never seemed to mind.

Well-behaved and well-trained dogs also went a long way toward keeping the peace with me, her dog-liker husband. Not only did I want a peaceful existence with my neighbors, but I also knew that having well-behaved dogs would make a calmer life inside our home. Mary Ellen and I had reached an unspoken agreement. She was responsible for the dogs' training, grooming, feeding, medical care, and exercising, as well as picking up toys and seeing that there was no dog hair about. I, in turn, supported her and helped with the dogs when she needed it, because I knew how important they were in her life. My passions were golf and fishing. She was understanding and supportive of my interests. She never tried to curtail them; rather, she encouraged me to pursue and enjoy them as often as possible.

I don't mean to imply that having dogs never bothered me. There were times when I was cranky or tired and whatever they were doing annoyed me, but Mary Ellen would recognize the situation and do her best to keep them away from me until I felt a little better. She saw to it that having dogs as pets did not disturb our life together or affect our relationships with our neighbors, and that worked for me. As with all couples, our marriage road was a little winding at times, and we encountered bumps and ruts here and there, but we were as committed to our marriage as Mary Ellen was devoted to her dogs, and so it worked because we wanted it to work.

Thinking back, I can recall one incident when having dogs definitely impacted our lives. About six years ago, we decided to downsize and look for a smaller home. We found a lovely residence in a small, exclusive gated community located inside a larger gated community. This house was perfect and just what we were looking for. On our visits to the house, we often saw people walking their dogs in the neighborhood. Some dogs were as large as a golden retriever. One owner regularly walked two

Siberian huskies. Believing the community was dog-friendly, we thought we would fit in nicely if we purchased a home there.

We had negotiated with the seller and were about to accept the offer that was on the table when the agent handling the transaction mentioned that the homeowners' association bylaws did not limit the number of dogs per home, but they did state that homeowners were limited to a *reasonable* number of dogs. She said it did not appear that our three dogs would be an issue. The bylaws also required that prospective owners be approved by the board of directors of the homeowners' association. Again, the real estate agent assured us that this was just a formality and no one was ever turned down.

So, at her direction, we sent a letter to the president of the homeowners' association. In the letter, we introduced ourselves as prospective homeowners and explained that I was a retired oral surgeon, my wife was a retired surgical nurse, and we presently had three dogs, but one had cancer and was not expected to live long. We also explained that our dogs were quiet and well behaved and that one was trained as a therapy dog. We included the names and phone numbers of two of our current neighbors for references.

It was not long before the agent received an e-mail from the homeowners' association president. His e-mail shocked everyone. Apparently we were not welcome with three dogs. He stated that he had contacted a number of members of the board, and not one would vote to allow us into their community.

The real estate agent and our attorney met with us. The agent, who was seasoned and experienced in real estate sales, said that ownership approval was a mere formality; she dealt with the issue all the time. Certainly there were reasons some buyers could be denied ownership, but having dogs was not one of them, especially when the bylaws placed no set restriction on the number of dogs. Our attorney chimed in, saying that clearly there was no legal standing to deny us ownership. He was more than confident that even if we had to go to court to press the issue, we would prevail.

But then they pointed out that although we could press the issue legally, take ownership, and move into the house, every time one of our dogs barked or took a pee on someone's grass, we would certainly hear about it. Further, it was apparent that we would not be welcomed by many of our neighbors, and so living in that community might not be very enjoyable. As much as we loved the house, this was not the life we were looking to live. We had no choice but to let it go and move on.

By then, our current house had sold, and we had about a month to vacate. Adjacent to the community that rejected us there was a similar community, and again we found a house that fit what we were looking for. The bylaws of this community limited each owner to two dogs. There wasn't much time to continue looking, and so we sent this community's president the same letter and asked that they consider making an exception to the two-dog rule, since one of our dogs had cancer and was not going to live very long.

The letter was passed on to the board of directors, and it didn't take long for them to tell us that they were happy to make an exception for the dogs and that we were more than welcome. We moved in, and immediately the neighbors sought us out to meet our dogs and make sure that we and our dogs felt welcome.

Mama Sam

ONE AFTERNOON I RETURNED HOME FROM MY usual golf game and found Mary Ellen getting ready to leave. "I am going to the shelter," she explained. "It is a sad situation. They have a thirteen-year-old female that a family dropped off. The family is homeless and living in their car and can't afford her anymore. She is so old that no one will even look at her when they come to the shelter. The shelter called out of desperation, because she is on the PTS list for tomorrow."

I suppose I could have asked Mary Ellen what she was going to do with this old female, but I was, after all, married to her, so I didn't need to ask.

Sometime later, Mary Ellen showed up with a small, gray-faced female. Our three big males stood in the doorway, waiting. Mary Ellen had her on a leash, and they proceeded to walk up the path until the tiny, thin old lady stood in front of the greeting party, looking them over. I observed the scene, imagining her as an old hag in a housecoat and slippers, a cigarette hanging from the corner of her mouth, saying, "So whatta you looking at? Get outta the way. You don't wanna mess with me."

With that, Alfie, Comet, and Charlie moved aside, and she sauntered past them into the house. They never uttered a sound.

She was tiny but had an attitude. She showed them that if

they had any ideas, they should forget it—she wasn't taking any of their crap. The next day she showed us she was the boss when we returned home and found she had pulled the toilet paper from all the rolls in all the bathrooms and deposited it all over the house. We had been TP'd. After that, we closed the bathroom doors when we left the house.

But in truth, Mama Sam (as we called her) was no problem to us in any way. If she wanted to sit where one of the other dogs was sitting, she just stood over him and he would move. Likewise, if she wanted the spot in the SUV where another dog was sitting, he got the message and found somewhere else to park his butt. When Charlie put on his swimming display, with Alfie and Comet joining in to create a ruckus, Mama Sam would step up on a chaise lounge, relax, and observe them with a bored look on her face. She always stayed on the periphery and never got into the mix of things. She was very good at playing the role of an elder who commanded a lot of respect, and consequently, the males never challenged or hassled her. Life was quiet over the next two years, after which she died peacefully of old age.

Before we moved to a restricted neighborhood we could have as many dogs as we wished. As a dog liker, I thought that bringing a fourth dog into our house would test the limits of my patience, but I must admit that Mama Sam was different. She touched my heart. When I saw her—old and gray and shuffling along—I was moved. I could have ordered her out and told Mary Ellen "Absolutely not—no more," but I knew that if I did she would be taken back to the shelter, and the following day she would be gone. Somehow I couldn't bring myself to do that. My basic human nature took over, and some inner compassion prevailed. It was unrelated to dogs and how much I liked them. In the end, I was glad I let her stay.

I remember another instance when things turned out differently. It was early in our marriage, and again we had three males at the time. They were all quiet, well behaved, and well trained. Life was peaceful, as they did not burden or disrupt us in any way. They got along wonderfully, and in truth, sometimes I hardly knew they were around.

Then one day I came home from the office, and when I opened the door, I saw not three but four faces greeting me. I paused and took a good look at nearest face. I did not recognize it, and in addition it looked odd. I looked more closely and realized it was holding two tennis balls in its mouth.

I found Mary Ellen in the kitchen. "What's with the new addition?" I asked.

"Oh, that's Cooper, a young male I brought in today," she said. "I thought I would keep him until I find the right home for him. He is a bit high-strung and wants to get into everything."

"Does he always carry two tennis balls in his mouth?"

"Well, earlier he was strutting around with *three* tennis balls."

I looked around. "How come there are toys all over the house?"

"Well, he takes them out one by one and deposits them all over. I'll get them picked up while you're changing."

As I went to my bedroom closet to change, I noticed that Cooper was leading the other three dogs around the house. It appeared he was now the head of the pack—and looking for trouble. Our three males seemed to be in awe of him. I was in the process of changing clothes in my closet when I noticed that one of the tassels from my Gucci loafers was lying on the floor. On closer inspection, I found that the other three had been chewed off as well. Needless to say, I was not happy!

I walked into the bedroom just as Cooper showed up and proceeded to jump on the bed. Our dogs knew better; jumping on the bed was not allowed. They just stood there and stared at him. I gave Cooper a firm "Off!" command, but it fell on deaf ears as he stood there looking at me, the two tennis balls bulging in his cheeks. Then he dropped them and barked at me. I called out for help: "Mary Ellen, you better get in here!"

I could hear her footsteps as she asked, "What is going on?"

At that point, Cooper—who was still on the bed—raised his leg and relieved himself. Then he picked up the two tennis balls and stood there to greet Mary Ellen as she entered the room.

I gathered myself, and without shouting, I said, "Take him and confine him to the laundry room. He is not going anywhere else in this house. Tomorrow when I come home, I want him gone. Not the following day or the day after. Tomorrow. I want him gone!"

This was one time in the marriage where the lines were drawn. Mary Ellen knew it, and she did not attempt to convince me otherwise. Nor did she protest, as she knew it was useless.

When I came home the following day, Cooper and his tennis balls had been placed with adopters on a trial basis. It was a young couple, and when informed that Cooper was untrained, prone to mischief, and maybe a little zany, they did not hesitate.

"Bring him over," the husband told Mary Ellen. "We are looking for an active dog."

From time to time after that, Mary Ellen would start a conversation with me by saying, "You will never believe what Cooper did."

"Now what did he do?" I would answer.

Mary Ellen would then proceed to tell me a story of some mischief and mayhem he had caused in his new home.

"How do the new owners feel about him?" I would ask.

"Oh, they are crazy about him," she would answer. "They think he is a riot."

As I have said repeatedly, dog lovers are different.

Changing the Mission

MARY ELLEN AND HER FELLOW GRININC BOARD members, Marcia and Linc, were getting burned out. All three had been rescuing dogs for many years, and the work was beginning to take its toll both physically and emotionally. They talked often about what to do, and over time a new mission emerged. GRININc would concentrate on special-needs dogs (those with medical issues) and older dogs, which were hard to place or even considered unadoptable. Special-needs dogs required continual medical care that was costly, and as a result these dogs were difficult to adopt out. In addition, prospective adopters did not want a dog whose best years were behind it and that most likely would be with them for only a year or two.

Mary Ellen, Marcia, and Linc came up with a solution for that problem: if some fosters would take these special-needs and older dogs and care for them until they passed away, GRININc would support the dogs financially for as long as they lived. GRININc had a list of fosters willing to do this; they were called "permanent fosters." All they were expected to do was provide a loving home and the basic necessities, and GRININc would take care of the rest.

Older and special-needs dogs comprised a small percentage of the dogs rescued and taken in each year. The bulk of the intakes were younger dogs that were easier to place. A group of GRINinc volunteers indicated that they would break away and start separate golden retriever rescues that would serve the needs of the younger dogs. These volunteers were fresh and eager and would do a good job. If GRINinc was contacted about younger dogs that did not fit into the new mission guidelines, then it would just refer them out. And so the mission of GRINinc changed, and two more golden rescues were formed.

A good example of a special-needs dog and permanent foster is Harley. He was brought into the rescue when he was five years old. He had developed Addison's disease, and his family could not afford the cost of his ongoing medical care. Several other golden rescues had turned him down, considering him unadoptable.

GRINinc decided that Harley deserved a second chance. Yes, all the testing and treatment involved with his medical care was expensive, but he was a sweetheart and a lover, with dark-brown eyes that melted the heart of everyone who met him. Jeri, one of GRINinc's volunteers, fell in love with Harley. She already had three goldens of her own, but she just could not turn Harley down. She wanted to foster him and give him all the comforts of home and all the love he could absorb. The rescue would pay all his medical bills. Harley had his ups and downs over the many years he was with Jeri, but for the most part his health remained good and he enjoyed life.

Sadly, while giving Harley a bath, Jeri experienced a ruptured brain aneurysm and passed away. Jeri's son and daughter-in-law, who lived with her and her dogs, wanted to keep Harley with them. By this time, he was a senior golden, and it would have been extremely difficult and stressful to move him; GRINinc's board members decided it was in Harley's best interest for him to stay with the family, and the rescue would continue to pay for all his medical care.

Harley lived another couple of years after Jeri's passing—until he was sixteen years old. It was comforting to the dog lovers in the rescue to know that when Harley crossed over the Rainbow Bridge, Jeri was there waiting for him. They were united once again.

Around that same time, GRINinc started an awards/grant program. Many rescues throughout the country are mom-and-pop organizations, usually run by a dog lover and a couple of volunteers devoted to dog rescue. Sometimes it is a one-woman operation that does it all. Some of these rescues are located in small, rural communities, and they do not have the financial resources available to the rescues in large metropolitan areas. They struggle because both funds and volunteers are in short supply. When small rescues like these take in a dog requiring a whole lot of medical care in order to recover, the veterinary costs for that one dog alone can exhaust their funds, which are meager at best.

GRINinc was looking for these situations. It spread the word through the Golden Retriever Club of America's National Rescue Committee that if a rescue was faced with unusually high veterinary costs in order to save a dog it had rescued, GRINinc would help with the finances. All that GRINinc required was that it be a golden retriever rescue and an IRS-approved 501(c)(3) public charity and that it submit an application detailing the dog's medical needs along with a financial report.

The GRINinc board reviewed the applications, which included reports from veterinarians involved in the dogs' care. Some dogs needed treatment for cancer or kidney failure or had other medical problems requiring ongoing care. Some had been hit by a car and needed surgery. Some needed cancerous growths removed, and others had bad knees or hips waiting for surgical correction. Regardless of the particulars, if lack of finances was preventing a dog from receiving treatment, GRINinc was there to help. Soon grant requests came in from all over the Southeast and as far away as West Virginia, many from small towns that were difficult to find on a map.

Sometimes board members reviewing an application had to contact the applying rescue because more information was needed, or they would call and talk to the treating veterinarian. After all their questions were answered, the board would decide on a dollar amount and send a check directly to the veterinarian so treatment could begin. If a rescue thought the dog was worth saving and was willing to do anything to save it, then GRINinc would help.

The grants varied from a few hundred to four or five thousand dollars, depending on the particulars of the case. The rescues receiving the awards would send GRINinc a photo of the dog and a short story to include in its newsletter. GRINinc named its awards/grant program the Golden Gifted Program. In time it would expand and become nationally recognized by the Golden Retriever Club of America's National Rescue Committee, which selected GRINinc for its annual Starfish Award in 2010.

GRINinc would need to continue to raise funds to support its new mission, and those fundraising efforts varied. Each Christmas season, for example, GRINinc volunteers would bring their goldens to Nordstrom and set up a table where shoppers could stop and pet the dogs and have their purchases wrapped in exchange for a donation. GRINinc called the event Wrapping for Gold.

Another fundraising program involved the automobile company Subaru, which each year has a national promotion during which it gives designated charities a donation for every Subaru sold at their local dealership. GRINinc was selected in the Naples area and received a donation for every auto sold at DeVoe Subaru, the local dealer. These and other fundraising programs needed to continue so that GRINinc could go forward with its new mission.

The GRINinc awards/grant program was expanding, the good work continued, and Mary Ellen, Marcia, and Linc were as busy as ever. They had newsletters to get out and other fundraisers to organize. There was one thing GRINinc could never give up, however: the rescue hotline. It served as the lifeline to dogs before and after they came to GRINinc.

Like the vast majority of rescues, GRINinc kept meticulous records. Consequently it had a huge computerized database with the name of every dog rescued, the date it was brought into the rescue, where it was fostered, and who finally adopted it. Each dog was also microchipped and given a special collar with a GRINinc tag. The dogs were never to be without their collar or tags; adopters were required to see that the dogs wore them at all times. Each tag had the GRINinc hotline phone number and the dog's GRINinc ID number.

Occasionally dogs got loose from their owners. That was understandable. A child leaves a door open or a dog wedges itself through a hole in the fence—it happens. These precautions ensured that anyone finding the dog could check the tag, call the GRINinc hotline, and provide the dog's GRINinc number, and Mary Ellen could go to the database and quickly identify the dog. The owner would be called and told where his or her dog was located and waiting for pickup. Mary Ellen usually ended these conversations by saying, "Let's not have that happen again."

Whenever I speak of microchips, I am reminded of Teddy, a rambunctious three-month-old goldendoodle who got curious and escaped from his yard. His family searched everywhere. They put up posters and offered a reward. They called veterinarians and shelters. They were hopeful that someone would call, because he was microchipped, but the call that they were waiting for never came. They were heartbroken.

Six long months went by, during which time the family took in another dog, a rescue that needed a new home. Then one day, Teddy's owner received a call from the local shelter. It had Teddy; the microchip has proven invaluable. Of course, Teddy's owner went to the shelter and was very happy to see him, but she hardly recognized him. When Teddy left, he'd had that full puppy-doodle coat and bright, dark eyes. This dog was skinny, with hardly any coat and very sad eyes. Certainly it was Teddy, but how the shelter had gotten him was another story. A local hoarder had been investigated, and all the dogs on her property had been confiscated by animal control. Teddy was among those poor dogs. Obviously the hoarder had been happy to find a high-value dog wandering around; never bothering to check for a chip or to see if he had a family out there somewhere, she immediately claimed him as her own.

While Teddy was receiving medical treatment for the many conditions he had developed, the family contacted GRINinc. They were distraught. They could not take Teddy back, as their new dog did not like other dogs. So they asked that the rescue find a loving forever home for Teddy. It was Christmastime, and a family that had just lost their golden was looking for another one to fill their hearts and home. Although Teddy was a doodle and not a golden retriever, they opted to drive many miles to visit him to see if there would be a connection. Although Teddy was far from looking like a golden, especially since he did not have any fur, they fell in love with his sweet, pleading brown eyes and took him home.

The following December, they sent a photo of Teddy by their Christmas tree. It showed a happy, sweet boy who looked like a healthy goldendoodle, with a paw crossed over his new Christmas toy. The pictures GRINinc had of Teddy revealed a remarkable transformation. In this case it was ultimately the microchip that saved Teddy and allowed the rescue to provide him with a new home and a new life.

It is quite common for adopters to send Mary Ellen pictures of the dogs she has placed. Usually, the adopters include them in their annual Christmas cards. Most often the dog and its family are posed in front of the Christmas tree, and so one Christmas Mary Ellen was surprised to open a card and find a picture of Casey resting on a sandy beach. Casey was a big red four-year-old who had recently been placed with a well-known Naples family. The rescue had found him on a farm; he was underweight and covered with ticks and fleas, with hardly any coat. Some time had passed, and in these pictures Casey had gone from a frail, sickly-looking golden to a handsome red boy sporting a beautiful coat and relaxing on a beach.

Mary Ellen came to find out that Casey's family had a private plane that they used to fly to the Bahamas from time to time, and they always took Casey with them. The airplane even had a special seat made just for him. Casey became very well known around the family's beautiful beachfront property in the Bahamas. He would hang out on the beach, lie down and rest with his owners, enjoy the sun, and even take part in beach parties as the guest of honor. No question—Casey hit it big. There would be no more life on the horse farm for him!

Savings Dogs and Souls

MARY ELLEN IS CONSUMED WITH THE WORK of GRINinc, but she still manages to find time for church activities, and her involvement with her church absorbs what little time she had left over from rescue. She couldn't squeeze anything else into her life. On Sundays she serves as a Eucharistic minister, assisting in the service. In addition, she spends one day a week touring the floors of the nearby hospital, visiting sick and ailing parishioners. A hospital is like home to Mary Ellen and just being there energizes her. As a nurse who had worked in a hospital, she experiences a certain level of comfort in that setting. She is familiar with the hospital's rules and inner workings, and she speaks their language. She is one of them.

Her skill as a Registered Nurse allows her to understand illness and suffering and what sick patients are experiencing. Because of her professional training, she is not bothered when she comes upon patients who were attached to bags of fluids and blood and have various tubes inserted into their bodies. Often she finds patients who are barely able to talk because they are sedated and filled with narcotics to alleviate their pain. Drawing up a chair, she sits and holds their hand and provides some comforting words and then prays with them. Since she has many patients to visit, she cannot stay long with any of them—just long enough to make the visit meaningful to this patient who is in need of comfort. Her experience as a hospital minister is more than fulfilling, and in many ways transforming. Mary Ellen found visiting those who were sick and hospitalized so rewarding that she felt compelled to expand and start an organized program just as she started her own dog rescue. The parish provided services to visit sick parishioners only when the family called and requested a visit, however she felt an organized program of trained ministers going to the hospital each day, checking the census and visiting each and every patient would be the most effective. She then sought volunteers from the parish who shared her compassion and commitment and trained them to in hospital ministry. She wrote a protocol for the new volunteers and arranged for them to accompany her until they were comfortable enough to do the visits alone. The response was all positive and the program has proven to be so successful a second hospital has now been added. Many of these hospitalized patients were fallen away Christians and had not been to church in a very long time. This was an opportunity for them to revitalize their faith. It helped many to revisit their religious convictions and to begin to pray and attend church regularly. Many were lost souls who needed help in finding their faith. Some were seriously ill and these prayerful visits gave them comfort and helped them reconnect with their religious beliefs. As the coordinator Mary Ellen is responsible for the scheduling and other aspects of the program to be sure it runs smoothly.

Mary Ellen had few compelling interests other than the rescue and the church. Combined, they took up her whole life. She was never into the country club scene. She was not a clubber. She did not play tennis, golf, or bridge, and in truth there was little time for her to pursue these activities. Two-hour lunches with the ladies and playing mah-jongg never appealed to her. As a consequence, my friends at the golf club would not see her for long periods of time and would ask about her.

"She is very busy," I would tell them.

"But what does she do with her time?" they would ask.

Initially I would give them a lengthy explanation of how her dog rescue and church work occupied most of her time and what that entailed, but that never seemed to satisfy some people. Some friends understood, and others did not. After a while, I gave up the explanations and simply told them, "She spends all her time saving dogs and souls."

It is not that we didn't have a social life. We dined out from time to time and attended club functions. But to a few friends, neighbors, and even family members, Mary Ellen was a little different, maybe a bit odd. Especially when they learned that she brushed her dogs' teeth every day.

Those who had their own passions understood what motivated her. They recognized the depth of her compassion and her need to provide comfort and joy to dogs and souls. In return, she always understood and supported their passions. When they held fundraisers to help the homeless, the needy, the disadvantaged, or some other social problem, she never hesitated to write a check. She wished she had enough time to volunteer for their causes, but she did not. There simply was no more time. Running GRINinc was akin to running a company, and she was the president who answered her own phone and got her own coffee.

We no longer have four dogs or the sprawling house with the adjacent, fenced-in half lot that allowed them to run free. We still live in the community with the two-dog limit and the downsized home. The two-dog limit is just fine for a dog liker like me. It is just what I was looking for: a *dog-liker* community. Mary Ellen is content with two dogs. She has our senior male, Casey, whom she has trained as a therapy dog, and a young female named Roxy. When she does manage to find some free time, Mary Ellen takes Casey on visits to a nearby rehabilitation facility, where he charms patients recovering from stroke or surgery.

Epilogue

I am eternally grateful to all the wonderful people in the world of dog rescue I've met and gotten to know, because dog lovers have influenced me in ways that I am just now beginning to understand. I have absorbed some of their empathy and kindness, and I'm a better person for it. They taught me that if you open your heart, you will be surprised to find how much room you have there. Although I have never completely made the transition from dog liker to dog lover, I was never considered a hopeless case, and the dog lovers in my life never gave up on me. Consequently, my wife and her friends continue to hold out hope that I will come around and be totally converted. They would like someday to say, "He is one of us—he is a dog lover."

Sandy and April continue their rescue work in Ohio, and Marcia and Linc have joined Mary Ellen as the mainstays of Golden Rescue in Naples, Inc. There are thousands more like them all over this country. They represent every breed and are tireless in their pursuits to save as many dogs as they can. These caring individuals are responsible for the rescue of countless numbers of dogs and giving them new homes and new lives; they serve as an inspiration for dog lovers everywhere. They can't save all the dogs in need, but they save as many as they can, never becoming disillusioned or discouraged by the sheer number needing their help. Instead, they continue to pursue their passion and bring joy and happiness to new owners. Their work is never finished as they follow their calling and their hearts.

Thinking of them, I am reminded of the starfish story:

> A young man was walking along the ocean and came to a beach where thousands and thousands of starfish had washed ashore. Farther along, he saw a young woman who was walking slowly and stooping often, picking up one starfish after another and tossing it gently into the ocean.
>
> "Why are you throwing starfish into the ocean?" he asked.
>
> "Because the sun is up and the tide is going out," she said, "and if I don't throw them farther out, they will die."
>
> "But, young lady, don't you realize there are miles and miles of beach with starfish all along it? You can't possibly save them all. You can't even save one-tenth of them. In fact, even if you work all day, your efforts won't make any difference at all."
>
> The young lady listened calmly and then bent down to pick up another starfish and throw it into the sea. "It made a difference to that one."

Printed in the United States
By Bookmasters